A.V.D. Honeyman

From America to Russia in Summer of 1897

A.V.D. Honeyman

From America to Russia in Summer of 1897

ISBN/EAN: 9783337298739

Printed in Europe, USA, Canada, Australia, Japan

Cover: Foto ©Andreas Hilbeck / pixelio.de

More available books at **www.hansebooks.com**

FROM AMERICA TO RUSSIA

IN SUMMER OF 1897

EDITED BY

A. V. D. HONEYMAN

PLAINFIELD, N.J.
HONEYMAN & COMPANY
1897

PREFACE.

THIS is the third volume in what is intended to be a series of annual books of travel, printed for private circulation among members of the H. P. T. parties to Europe and their friends. It will be found not to fall below previous ones in interest. The Tour described includes Norway and Sweden, as well as Russia, in its scope. The contributors' names are affixed to each article.

A. V. D. H.

TABLE OF CONTENTS.

		Page.
I.	New York to Antwerp,	9
II.	Coaching: Antwerp to Worcester,	15
III.	Coaching: Worcester to Coventry,	23
IV.	Coaching: Coventry to Oxford,	32
V.	England to Norway,	40
VI.	Along the Norwegian Coast,	51
VII.	Across Norway,	61
VIII.	Across Sweden,	66
IX.	In Stockholm,	79
X.	Finland and St Petersburg,	88
XI.	The Old Russian Capital,	98
XII.	Our Longest Railway Journey,	115
XIII.	Berlin and Its Environs,	122
XIV.	A Day in Amsterdam,	137
XV.	Homeward Bound,	152

ILLUSTRATIONS.

	Facing Page.
On the West Gotha Canal, Sweden, (frontispiece.)	
Oscar II, King of Sweden and Norway,	8
Coaching in Oxfordshire,	20
The Lodge,	24
Starting from the Red Horse Inn,	26
Coaching: Between Kenilworth and Coventry,	34
Lincoln Cathedral—West Front,	42
A Norway Fjord,	44
The Steamer "Neptun,"	48
A Norwegian Home,	52
Molde,	54
A Norwegian Stolkjaerre,	58
King Oscar's Summer Chateau,	62
The Holmenkollen Hotel, Christiania,	64
Street View in Gothenburg,	70
A Fjord Late in the Afternoon,	80
The King's Garden, Stockholm,	86
Russian Drosky and Driver,	90
The Singing Deacon of St. Isaac's,	96
Cathedral of the Assumption, Moscow,	104
Cathedral of St. Basil, Moscow,	108
The King of Bells, Moscow,	114
The Young Holland Queen,	150

"The bee, though it finds every rose has a thorn, comes back loaded with honey from its rambles, and why should not other tourists do the same.—"*Haliburton.*

Oscar II., King of Sweden and Norway.

Born Jan. 21, 1829; ascended the joint throne of Sweden and Norway 1872, succeeding his brother, Charles XV. He is known as a wise and intellectual monarch, endowed with much taste for and accurate knowledge of art, science, poetry and music.

FROM AMERICA TO RUSSIA.

I.

NEW YORK TO ANTWERP.

ON the afternoon of Wednesday, June 30, 1897, promptly at half past four o'clock, the S. S. "Kensington," of the Red Star line, drew out from her pier with the Honeyman Party, twenty-one in number, among her full quota of passengers. Gradually the group of friends, waving good-bye with their handkerchiefs, faded away in the distance, and the wide separation of two continents and the absence of many days seemed to be crowded into the feelings of a moment. It is a sensation to which even an old traveler never becomes entirely hardened. Slowly the steamer passed down the Bay and through the

Narrows, and pushed her nose oceanward. And now new thoughts had begun to engross our attention in the direction of prospect and anticipation, for these suggest uncertainties and untried experiences.

There are three leading factors which enter into a sea voyage, and contribute largely to its comfort or discomfort. These are the steamer, the passenger list and the weather. It is difficult to say which is the most important. Any one of these may do much to ruffle or to smooth one's peace of mind.

As for the steamer, much may be said in praise. We found her comfortable, the service courteous and attentive; and a steadier deck in a sea one could scarcely hope to tread. When the "Kensington" reached port there were many who expressed the wish that they might some time cross in her again.

As for the company on board, a pleasant party of our own made it possible for us to be quite independent. However, among the other passengers there were many agreeable people who added greatly to the pleasure of the voyage, and it was not long before an unusual degree of sociability prevailed throughout the ship. Although many of the "H. P's." were unknown to one another at the start, there was an early opportunity for making the beginning of an exceedingly pleasant acquaintance. Through the prearrangement of the Manager, places had been so secured that the members of the party were able to sit together at the first table, and we soon met for our first meal.

Ah, the first meal on an ocean steamer! What qualities of soul it calls into play! Self-confidence and prudence go hand in hand, and smiling heroism covers up a lurking suspicion with reference to the probabilities of such another unanimous meeting, for wind and wave have not yet settled down to work. Joyfully the poet sings,

"O'er the glad waters of the dark blue sea,
 Our thoughts as boundless and our souls
    as free;"

only that depends. It depends upon circumstances, for there are circumstances at sea that may annihilate all poetry, set a decided limit to thought and make the fettered soul sigh for freedom. As one of our number expressed it, for a time he felt as though he did not know whether he was "comin' or gwine." But this was not so with most of the party, and with him only for a short time, for the voyage was on the whole an easy and pleasant one. Occasionally there was a little wind with rain and roughened sea, but not sufficient to make it a stormy passage.

So the days slipped by, as days will both on sea and land. Time passed rapidly. Hours were restfully spent, as, wrapped in rugs, we reclined in our steamer chairs, dozing or reading, as the fancy seized us. Things there always are to interest one—a passing vessel heralded by the toot of the lookout's horn, signaling port or starboard; the changing cloud effects, which, with nothing to interrupt the view, unfold with kaleidoscopic variety and exhibit ever new beauty. Time is employed pleasantly and profitably in conversation. The steamer from its "beginning," as one lady styled it, to the stern, offers ample room for restlessness to work itself off in exercise. And the bugle call has almost always an agreeable and inviting sound for the ears of every one.

This voyage was especially marked by one event. Independence Day was spent at sea. Falling on a Sunday, it was appropriately observed by the officiating clergyman praying for the Queen of England and the Prince of Wales; and by an elaborate dinner in which Independence pudding, Fourth of July pie and firecrackers, furnished by our Manager, figured prominently. And a further celebration was held on the following evening, when an excellent concert was given and fireworks were displayed—a novel and beautiful sight at night time in mid-Atlantic. Twice the passengers assembled in the saloon for an evening's entertainment, and on each occasion an "Honorable" member of the H. P. T. presided.

In this delightful manner the days of our voyage passed all too swiftly, until on the evening of Friday, July 9, about ten o'clock, the light on one of the Scilly Islands was sighted. Our thoughts now began to anticipate port. Saturday dawned a beautiful day, which was, you may be sure, fully appreciated, as it afforded a good opportunity for enjoying the passage through the Channel. Sails and funnels became more frequent. The English coast was kept most of the time in sight. We passed very close to the Isle of Wight, and late in the evening the lights of Folkestone, then of Dover and Calais, became visible.

On Sunday morning we witnessed a transformation scene. While on board, shore clothes almost destroyed personal identity, without the vessel it was no longer open sea, but the banks of the Scheldt hemming us in on both sides. Flushing had been passed early in the morning, and now we were slowly winding our way up the river. Long shall we remember the quaint and picturesque view that greeted our eyes as we appeared on deck that last morning—the dikes, strong and well built, suggesting that the familiar story of the boy who kept back the flood with his finger needed the attention of the higher criticism; the queer Dutch windmills lazily turning in the gentle wind; the straight rows of trees lining the highways; the odd little farm houses, the upper parts of which were alone visible, the remainder being hidden by the dikes; and now and again the Dutch peasantry, men and women, in the hayfields, taking advantage of the bright sunny morning to toss and rake the new-mown hay.

At eleven o'clock the steamer was at her dock in Antwerp. After going through the usual ordeal with the customs officers, we proceeded to the Hotel du Courrier, and so completed the first stage of our journey.

WILLIAM RUSSELL BENNETT.

II.

COACHING: ANTWERP TO WORCESTER.

A SHORT drive brought us to the Grand Hotel du Courrier; then followed a few hours' rest in a room which looked out on the pretty court garden.

The Cathedral chimes at Antwerp ring every quarter of an hour, and so speedily attract to the Notre Dame the stranger who hears their musical notes. At five we went to the organ service. The famous Rubens pictures, alas, were covered, but others had seen them earlier in the day. The side chapels were filled with devout worshipers.

We admired Van der Voort's exquisitely carved wood pulpit. The figures which support it stand in an enclosure, which has a stairway on each side. Above are carved medallions. The canopy is raised by cupids.

At the top, an angel leans down, blowing a trumpet. A dove hovers in the center. The branches of a tall tree reach as high as the canopy, and cover the sides of the stairways with their foliage. Peacocks and other birds disport themselves, at intervals.

The wrought-iron well canopy of Quinten Massys, the blacksmith artist, stands near the Cathedral.

The next morning a visit was made to St. Paul's. The Calvary, which is in a grotto-like garden, was visited first. Figures of the prophets stand on each side, surrounded by lovely flowers. An angel holds a shield, showing the heart, pierced hands and feet of our Lord. The Calvary is at the end of the garden. The figure of Christ on the cross is at the top. A skeleton lies below, while two angels, one on each side, point to the Saviour. Below is a "Pieta." There is also a cave which represents the Holy Sepulcher. The beautifully carved confessionals in this church are the work of Quellyn. "The Scourging of our Lord," by Rubens, was unveiled by the guide. On the opposite side is the "Council of Popes." The fifty legends of the rosary are on the left side, near the entrance. Above the doorway is the sculptured figure of the Virgin, holding a rosary in her hand. In a side chapel are carvings representing the different stations of the cross.

We then went to the Musée Royal, which is filled with fine paintings of the Flemish school. There is an exquisite group of angels by Memling, designed for an altar piece. They form a choir and are in a carved wood setting, which fills one whole side of the room. Here one sees Van Dyck's masterpiece, "The Crucifixion," Rubens' "Crucifixion of Christ Between Two Thieves;" his "Dead Christ," his "Adoration of the Magi;" exquisite landscapes of the two Ruysdaels, portraits by Hals, true Holland types; "La Dame Hollandaise," a placid gentlewoman in broad white ruff and cap. There are characteristic peasant scenes by Brenghel, Teniers, Steen and Vinckboons, showing the merrymakings of the kermesse, the rustic wedding, and scenes in the village inn.

Rembrandt has two portraits. Van Eyck's "Saint Catherine" sits in front of a Gothic edifice, her voluminous skirts filling the whole foreground. There are fine examples of Memling, Massys, Mostaert, de Vos, Van der Weyden, Van Ostade, Van de Velde, Wynants, and others, too numerous to mention.

In the afternoon there was a long drive

through the city. The arms of Antwerp, as I learned, are two hands. The monument, with the figure throwing the hand, and the Flemish device "hand werpen," commemorates the legend of the giants, Antigonus, who cut off the hands of those who refused to pay the toll that he exacted.

Another monument commemorates throwing off the Spanish yoke in 1706. The base shows the shackles thrown off by the hands sculptured above. In the center is a medallion of the first burgomaster, and, above that, a figure of victory with a torch.

We saw the town hall, and, nearly opposite, the house in which Charles V. was born. At the top is a fine equestrian statue in gilt.

We passed the Flemish and French theaters. The latter has busts of the French composers and dramatists.

We went through lovely parks and past many quaint, interesting houses. At seven P. M. we drove to the boat, which was to take us across the Channel to Harwich.

As we left it Antwerp seemed like a jewel in a lovely setting, framed by the sunset clouds of orange chrome and rose pink. On the opposite shore the rushes waved high and green.

The passage to England was a calm one. At

Coaching   On the Road in Oxfordshire.

six the next morning we landed, passed through the custom-house at Harwich, and at seven took the train for London. Eight o'clock found us at the Liverpool street station, where we had breakfast; then, taking the underground railway to Paddington station, we were soon en route for Oxford.

After lunching at the King's Arms Hotel we mounted the coaches and began the trip for which so many of us had looked forward with unusual zest—the coaching tour of five days—and it was so satisfying and inspiring that one regrets that a few pages only must suffice for its description. The day was perfect, cool, clear, invigorating. Mr. Franklin, Jr., whose father formerly managed the reins of the leaders, took his seat on the front box, the mourning band on his arm indicating that the soul of the good man who was not with us had gone to its eternal reward. To us who had never seen either there was no knowledge of the difference it occasioned, but to our Manager and some of his fellow-travelers it must have been a scene whose pleasure was mingled with profound sorrow.

The steeds started to the crack of the whip and we bowled along over roads of flint as smooth as a drum-head for miles and miles, and the first stop was at Blenheim, to see if we could enter the Duke of Marlborough's estate. Happily we could not only enter, but we could do more; we had the unusual delight of joining an English party of lady school teachers and being shown through the palace itself.

The gates of the castle are of massive gilt and bronze, and show the coat of arms on each side. The Duchess, it is said, may wear this, but not the crest. After entering the castle the guide drew our attention to the massive lock of the door, an exact copy of one in Warsaw. In the gallery above are portraits of Queen Anne and different members of the Marlborough family. Each room has portraits of the beautiful Duchesses. The third Duchess is especially lovely. The portrait of the present Duchess shows a piquant face, brunette in type, a slender figure in a flowing white robe, a wand in one hand. The last room shown had a magnificent organ. Here are busts of the present Duke and Duchess. In the chapel is the monument erected by the first Duchess in memory of her husband and two sons.

Then followed a two hours' beautiful drive to Chipping Norton, where we left the coaches for the day, in order to go by rail to Worcester, a place we reached at half past seven. Eight o'clock found us comfortably settled at the Unicorn Hotel.

The next morning we visited Worcester Cathedral. The organ was playing and the guide showed its three divisions, which look like three different instruments. The Cathedral as a whole was restored in 1857, as it was rapidly going to decay. Its shape is a double cross. Although ravaged by three fires, it always rose, phœnix-like, from its ashes. The Norman and Perpendicular styles of architecture are the most marked. A stained glass window in the central tower represents "The Creation." The pulpit of the nave has sculptured scenes from the Bible; and here are also many interesting monuments. The combination of different marbles and alabaster is exquisite. There is a magnificent, richly carved screen; also thirty-seven unique stalls.

King John is buried at Worcester, and the sculptured effigies of the numerous bishops who rest there are recumbent on stone slabs. They wear the episcopal robes. In the crypt we saw how the carved columns had once been covered with plaster, so that the lovely designs were completely concealed, and, perhaps unsuspected until after the Restoration.

The Unicorn was a most comfortable hotel, and we voted Worcester a place of sufficient interest to have remained longer.

LIZZIE J. STODDARD.

III.

COACHING: WORCESTER TO COVENTRY.

WORCESTER was left with considerable regret because of the intrinsic beauty of its Cathedral, especially the interior. It is thought by some good judges to have as beautiful an interior as any English Cathedral except Canterbury, and with a groined roof which no other can match. Not having seen Canterbury I cannot vouch for the accuracy of the full statement, but the general effect of the roof, windows, arches and pillars made a more entrancing impression upon me than either the Cathedrals of York, Ely, Lincoln or Peterborough. An hour's meditation every day beneath such a vaulting, where, amid great simplicity, there is the magnificence of true art, must be stimulating to any human soul.

The railway was taken at this point back to Chipping Norton, where the coaches were in readiness for the day's drive to Stratford.

Some of us felt that this day's drive was in many respects the most delightful of any of the coaching tour. The views of the Malvern Hills in the distance, the unusual atmosphere for July, so clear and bracing, the constantly changing panorama of views, at times extending to twenty miles in either direction, made the day one long to be remembered.

The noon-hour was spent at Shipston-on-Stour, at the "George Inn," where we had a royal good time, especially at the dinner.

In the afternoon we passed what was voted to be "the handsomest lodge in England." It was only a small house, at the gateway leading into a large estate, but it was embowered in vines and roses. Its shape was something like that of a beehive, but everything about it— the garden, the setting of woods, the lodge itself—made us all, as we first viewed it from a distance, almost clap hands with delight. Of course we dismounted and went to see it. There was a charming old lady in charge, who made no objection to the inspection of the premises, nor to our taking away handsfull of the beautiful roses. Each of our amateur

The Lodge.

The same which was voted by the H. P. T. party as the most beautiful they had seen in England. Ten of the party appear in the picture.
(*Photo. by M. Estil*)

photographers had a snapshot at the lodge, and we will long carry the picture of it in the gallery of English memories.

Stratford-on-Avon has been so often described that it seems only necessary to say that we did the usual things which every visitor to the home and haunts of Shakespeare must do. We visited his birthplace, the George W. Child's Fountain, New Place (where the immortal bard had written his plays and where he died), the Grammar School, Trinity Church, the Anne Hathaway cottage, Town Hall, and similar spots of local interest.

> "Here his first infant lays, sweet Shakespeare sung;
> Here the last accents faltered on his tongue."

Some of the party boated by moonlight on the Avon, while others had a pleasant converse in the evening with the interesting landlady of the Red Horse Inn, who always takes the best of care of her guests. The Red Horse dining-room, with its memories of Washington Irving and William Winter, had been that very afternoon the place where Mrs. Mary Anderson de Navarro had lunched, and our Mrs. D. was fortunate enough to be given "William Winter's room" for the night. Probably all of us slept in beds which had been occupied at one time and another by some of the greatest men and women in England, for the Red Horse dates back as a hostelry to a fairly ancient period, and the present proprietor, Mr. Shelbourne, seems specially gratified to see his American friends, of whom he has a large and increasing number. I am always fond of this hotel, especially because of its quaint engravings and comfortable rooms.

Next day we were off for Warwick, not by the direct road, but by way of Hampton Lucy. Here we temporarily lost our way, but had in consequence an interesting experience with some school-children. The fact was we did not want to go to Hampton Lucy village, but to Charlecote Park, in its vicinity. We probably passed on the way the location of the house where Shakespeare's good friends, John and William Combe, resided, and where the poet must have spent many pleasant hours. When we did reach the park, we found it to be an estate which must have been glorious in its day, but was now chiefly beautiful because of its enormous old trees and wide stretches of fields, and it is still, as in olden days, full of domesticated deer.

It was in this park where it is said Shake-

Starting from the Red Horse Inn.

This hotel is the one in Stratford-on-Avon, long famous through the writings of Washington Irving, William Winter and others. The picture represents the first coach of the H. P. T. party about to start out for Charlecote Park, Warwick, Kenilworth and Coventry.

(*Photo. by M. Estil.*)

speare engaged in stealing deer from its owner, Sir Thomas Lucy. For this he was prosecuted, and, it is recorded, took his revenge by writing a caustic ballad now lost, probably his first essay in poetry. Be this as it may, Shakespeare knew every nook and corner of these woods, and when he wrote the "Merry Wives of Windsor," and possibly had Sir Thomas in mind in his character of Justice Shallow, he had at least stored up in memory beautiful images of days gone by when Charlecote Park was jocund with voices of youth and when England was more "merrie" with revelries and mischief-making than it has ever been since.

Charlecote House was built in 1558. It forms three sides of a quadrangle; is not particularly handsome nor imposing, though strictly Elizabethan and with various ornamental features which excite one's attention. If it were more closely shut in amid the old gnarled oaks and beeches, its effect would be finer, but it is rather out in the open and lacks the real picturesqueness of some other English halls. We were charged a fee for the privilege of passing through this place, a reminder to us that the present lords of England are not so wealthy that they can afford to open their estates to passersby without a contribution box.

At Warwick the horses were put out at the Warwick Arms, a hotel not at all satisfactory in its charges, though attractive within, and then a visit was made to the Beauchamp Chapel, to see the tomb of Dudley, Earl of Leicester, and the Earl of Warwick. Warwick Castle, the finest of its type in England, we discovered, to our regret, could not be visited, because the premiers of the various English colonies, who were on a visit to London to attend the Queen's Jubilee, had been invited this day by the Earl of Warwick to a garden party within his grounds. As we drove by the gate of the castle after luncheon, on our way to Kenilworth, we saw the nobility entering, watched by hundreds of English people who lined the way.

From Warwick to Leamington is a short two miles. Leamington looked fresh, handsome and thoroughly attractive for a summer residence. We passed directly through, stopping only five minutes to taste the mineral waters from one of the springs, and then took that remarkably beautiful road from Leamington to Coventry, by the way of Kenilworth, which has been so often described as "the prettiest drive in England." I do not altogether agree with this statement, but as the road is perfectly level, and hard and smooth as a floor, the country on each side fertile, and as almost the entire distance the way is lined with a row of stately limes and elms, I admit it would be very difficult to find other roads more charming.

Just outside of Warwick is Guy's Cliff, of considerable note, but though I have passed this spot a number of times, have never left the road and driven in to see it. This omission of duty I hope some day to supply.

At Kenilworth the same quiet ruins, so covered with dense ivy that from any point of view they are entrancing, still rest on the little hill outside of the town. Here the Earl of Leicester so royally entertained Queen Elizabeth that even Sir Walter Scott's pen paused to take time to irradiate the event with a prolonged description of its glories. It is one of the most lovely places in England for a picnic, or for a visit on a bright afternoon. Perhaps we spent two hours strolling about the ruins and upon the walls, and reclining about the grass, with our minds turned back to the days of chivalry. It was no difficult task to re-people the place with knights and courtiers and bishops, and all the ladies of the court of Elizabeth, who trooped hither in coaches and on horseback to enjoy the merry dinners of the favorite Earl.

I see now the incoming pageant on that memorable 9th of July, 1575! The Queen came, attended by thirty-one barons, besides all her ladies of court and four hundred servants. Six trumpeters "clad in long garments of sylk," to quote from the chronicler of the time, "who stood upon the wall of the gate, with their silvery trumpets of five foot long, sounded a tune of welcome." There were floating islands, water nymphs and genii, poets to read poetry and players to act plays, tilts, tournaments, deer hunts, bear and bull-bating, Italian rope-dancers, bridal ceremonies, merry dancing and "tables loaded with sumptuous cheer." I fancy that young Will Shakespeare, with the other boys of the vicinity, was attracted to the spot and at least peered through the gate to see these royal puppets move.

Seven miles northeast of Kenilworth lies Coventry. When we neared the latter place there was the first appearance of rain since we arrived in England. In the west and northwest the clouds were heavy and there came lightning and thunder. There were gusts of wind, with flying dust, and presently over fields the rains descended, and came nearer and nearer. But it kept away from over head. England was in need of rain and we were pleased that at least toward Worcestershire some farmers were benefited by the shower, but Coventry remained dry as a bone. We were landed at the King's Head Hotel without a drop upon us, and after the evening meal had a ten miles' tramway journey through and out of the city to Bedworth and return, and then went to bed with the image of Peeping Tom peering from above our windows.

A. V. D. Honeyman.

IV.

COACHING: COVENTRY TO OXFORD.

WE reached the King's Head Hotel, Coventry, at five o'clock, and first saw the bust of "Peeping Tom" peering from an adjoining window. He was a tailor who, according to the legend, was struck blind while looking at Lady Godiva as she rode through the city. Her husband, Leofric, imposed very heavy taxes on the people, and as there was but one condition on which he would remit them, she rode through the city covered only by her long hair.

I soon went to St. Michael's, a most interesting old church. Two of its windows are five hundred years old. They were shattered by a cannon ball when Cromwell tried to blow up the church, but have been restored. The fragments are leaded together so that the tiny pieces look like a veritable mosaic. The exterior is beautiful. A fine figure of a crusader stands high up in one of the niches on the left hand side. The carved roses and angels above the lower windows are exquisite.

Opposite is St. Mary's Guildhall, where Mary, Queen of Scots, was imprisoned for nine months. Her prison is behind the altar, and is reached by a winding flight of worn stone steps. It is lighted by two small windows. The adjoining room has a litter of books and a large picture of Bacchus and Ariadne.

Just before entering the Hall one sees a large, rudely carved statue, a relic of the Queen's crosses. The Hall, which is built of oak, is filled with portraits of Queen Mary, Queen Caroline, and the different Georges. A wonderful piece of tapestry covers one end of the room.

A small room adjoining contains the statue of Godiva, a lovely nude figure with hair flowing below her knees. A painting in a room adjoining the prison represents her on horseback, according to tradition. An underground room contains the charters and seals of the Kings of England.

Before leaving Coventry a visit was made to

the Old Women's Home. We entered a court, and on each side were the carved walls of a quaint building dating back five hundred years. There is a lovely garden at the end of the court. Each old lady has a tiny suite of rooms, nicely furnished, clean and bright, and filled with souvenirs, which they were eager to exhibit. All seemed contented and happy. As we passed out we were each given a few flowers from the garden.

A few hours later we left the coach to visit Stoneleigh Abbey, the seat of Lord Leigh. We drove through a long, rambling lane, bordered on each side with fine old trees. On entering we had a glimpse of the cloisters, which have been restored. A fine portrait of the present Lord Leigh hangs above the mantel in one room. It represents him as he was in his prime, thirty-five years ago. The portrait of his wife, as a young girl, hangs in the dining-room. There are many interesting portraits in the corridors. The chapel, where the family have private worship, contains a beautiful altar painting. In the gallery above is a marble medallion of the Virgin, clasping the head of Christ (Canova's). Another room contains a copy of Dürer's "Christ,' and an original painting near it.

Coaching: Between Kenilworth and Coventry.

On the right is an English forest; on the left, the usual hawthorne hedgerow and the trees of an estate. Between the road proper and the hedge will be seen, first, the bridal path, and, second, a wider footpath. These are completely-built, model public roads, the like of which we do not yet have in America. (*Photo. by M. Estil.*)

There is a Van Dyck portrait of Charles I., which has been restored. It was once sent away for repairs, when the discovery was made that the original canvas had been painted over. Another room had an exquisitely carved ceiling. All the chairs were delicately embroidered or painted. His lordship was absent and therefore we were permitted, through the courtesy of his intelligent housekeeper, to see the mansion.

We then drove to Warwick Castle, the first glimpse being that of its ivy-clad towers. Reaching there, after a luncheon at the Woolpack Inn, we passed on foot through a walled path, banked on each side with ivy and ferns. There are noble trees the whole distance. We climbed Guy's Tower, with its two hundred and fifty spiral, stone steps. From the top we could see the winding course of the Avon, which runs beside the Castle, and the three counties of Worcestershire, Oxfordshire and Gloucestershire. Gorgeous peacocks walked on the lawn. The flower beds near the greenhouse have each a red maltese cross in the center. From the garden there is a fine view of two magnificent Lebanon cedars; none of us saw finer in all our journeyings.

Hadrian's vase stands on a broad pedestal

in the center of the greenhouse. It was found at Hadrian's villa, near Rome. There are acanthus leaves around the base; vine tendrils form the handles; and their branches and fruit twine about the vase. On one side are satyrs with a lion skin spread below them; on the other is a beautiful head in profile between two satyrs.

On entering the Castle, Cromwell's death mask was one of the first objects seen. The guide remarked that as the Earl of Warwick had been on good terms with Cromwell, he had kept his castle. A corridor, lined with armour and weapons, also contains portions of Cromwell's armor.

Raphael's "Assumption" hangs over the mantel in the Red Drawing Room. Here, also, is an exquisite table, inlaid with lapis lazuli, once the property of Marie Antoinette.

The Gilt Drawing Room has Rubens' "Loyale" over the mantel. The Cedar Room is filled with Van Dycks. The portraits of the Brignolia family, mother and child, came from Genoa. The portrait of Nell Gwynne, above the doorway, is by Lely. Queen Anne's room has her portrait by Kneller, above the mantel. The massive bed is hung with crimson velvet and gold, and there is a richly embroidered coverlet. Her trunk, a tiny one with brass initials, is in this room.

A portrait of Henry VIII., by Holbein, hangs over the mantel in the Countess's boudoir. The same room contains his portrait "when a good little boy," as the guide facetiously observed. Here are also Holbein's portraits of Anne and Mary Boleyn.

The walls of the Oak Room are about eight feet thick. This forms wide recesses for the windows, and the arch above each is carved in vines and flowers. The walls of the Banqueting Hall are hung with magnificent antlers. One side is filled with suits of armor. Oliver Cromwell's helmet hangs here, and Richard Neville's mace.

In Beauchamp Chapel, at Warwick, we saw the tomb of the first Earl of Warwick, a recumbent, bronze-gilt figure; also the tomb of the wicked Earl of Leicester and his third wife, Letitia, and that of their child, whom the Earl caused to be murdered, because of his deformity. Opposite is the tomb of his brother, the Earl of Dudley, called the "Good Earl."

We went into the little oratory up the stone steps, worn smooth by the feet of penitents, and looked at the exquisite roof carvings, each fan being a separate stone. In the church we also saw the recumbent figures of the first Earl and his wife, he wearing the garb of a crusader.

Next came the final day's coaching to Oxford, and a royal day it was. Every day of the drive had been perfect and the last no less so than the others. And now we were to say farewell to the lovely English meadows, fields of poppies, the fragrant rows of lindens, the oaks, elms and larches, the willows which bordered the Avon, and the quaint, picturesque stone cottages covered with ivy. We were to leave the comfortable English inns. The fierce and lobster-like "Red Lion" of Banbury was to be a thing of the past.

A sign hanging in front of one of the last inns passed showed a buxom young woman in a blue and yellow costume. With shield in one hand, trident in the other, she leaned her head against the English flag, planted her sandaled feet firmly on the sand, and looked on the expanse of indigo blue water as though she defied anyone to dispute the right of Britannia to rule the seas. This was our last stop for the thirsty ones until we entered Oxford, when of a sudden came a mild rain, which somewhat, but only slightly, interfered with a long ride through the "city of colleges."

Here the members of former H. P. T. parties visited the grave and paid their respects to the memory of good William Franklin, the former owner of our coaches and horses; the man who, as our Manager said, " had conducted them over hundreds of miles of rural England, without an error of judgment, or a flaw perceptible in his sweet and kindly temper"; and they grieved that he was no more, while remembering that "the memory of the just is blessed."

LIZZIE J. STODDARD.

V.

ENGLAND TO NORWAY.

O N arriving at the Liverpool street station in London bound for Norway, the H. P. T. party was reinforced by the addition of five more members, but we were extremely sorry to lose one, the Rev. Mr. Bennett. Total number now, twenty-five.

We left London for Lincoln at five-thirty, and rode through a delightful country full of lovely fields of thrifty grain. The landscape in many places is flat, reminding one strongly of Holland. The little stations on the way where the train stopped were exceedingly pretty, and at one we saw a quantity of large baskets filled with delicious looking strawberries. There was a magnificent sunset, the sun being a brilliant red and just above there was a dark cloud that gradually sank over it and was tinged with the gorgeous hue.

Several windmills appeared on our way to Lincoln, and they always add materially to the beauty of the scenery.

When we arrived at the White Hart Hotel, in Lincoln, we were dusty, and were glad to reach such a home-like place. Of course we received a warm welcome from Miss Barton, the landlady, who knew many of the party personally and was ready to greet with special smiles those of us who had been there before. It was refreshing to see her bright face again. She served us a delicious dinner, but as we had charming meals when we were here before it was no better than was expected. There was plenty of fruit and the table was beautifully arranged, as it was two years ago. Soon after arrival we heard the rich and measured tones of a bell striking the hour of ten; this was undoubtedly "Big Tom." Some of us went out to see what we could of the Cathedral in the night, but it was too dark to see it to good advantage.

A rainy morning next day, but in spite of the rain we all went sight-seeing, and first to the Cathedral. Lincoln Cathedral was built in 1074, but what with fire and earthquake it has undergone many changes since. It is by no means rich in monuments, the sepulchral brasses, of which it contained a large number, having been taken up by Parliamentary soldiers in 1644. There are, however, several monuments left commemorating the death of noted individuals. The entire length of the Cathedral is 481 feet, the nave being 215 feet long and with the aisle 80 feet wide; the interior area of the entire building being 57,200 square feet. The height of the central tower is 271 feet and the height of each of the western towers 206 feet. One can get an idea of the size of the Cathedral from these dimensions. The bell known as "Great Tom of Lincoln" hangs in the central tower. It was recast in 1835, weighs over five tons, is 6 feet high and 21 feet in circumference at its base.

Lincoln is a good-sized city having a population of 40,000, and has many quaint sights described in other volumes of this series, so I will not detain the reader here further.

On our way from Lincoln to Hull, where we are to take the steamer for Bergen, we passed a great many towns and a large number of cattle grazing. Here again we saw windmills, but not as many as we counted later in our journey from Berlin to Amsterdam. Pretty canals and lovely winding rivers diversified the scenery. We stopped at Dorchester, a quaint

Lincoln Cathedral—West Front.

Lincoln has a population of 40,000, and on a hill in its centre is located the famous Cathedral, founded in the Eleventh Century; a structure "crystallized in mid-air by the wand of a magician, dripping solid splendor on every side."

old town, and had lunch and then rolled on some distance farther to beautiful Hull, a seaport town on the North Sea. We wished to stay here for at least one day that we might have a better view of it.

Of the ecclesiastical edifices at Hull the most notable are the Church of the Holy Trinity, a beautiful, ornate, Gothic structure, the transept of which is the oldest English brick building in the country; and St. Mary's Church, Lowgate, one-half of which was removed to make room for the mansion-house of Henry VIII., who occasionally resided here. The most important educational establishments are the Hull Grammar School, and Trinity House School where 36 boys receive a nautical education. An equestrian statue of William III. stands in the market place and a statue of Wilberforce, who was born in 1759. A new west dock which greatly increases the accommodation for shipping was opened in 1869. A town hall and a new exchange were opened in 1866. Hull has a population of 160,000.

On our arrival in Hull we took 'busses to go to the wharf, where we embarked in a tender for the steamer the "Eldorado." The steamer proved to be well appointed and very comfortable.

That night and next day we were on the North Sea on our way to Bergen. The sea was a little rough next morning and there were few ladies out to breakfast. On the whole our sail proved a delightful one and I enjoyed it to the full. The sunset at night was of the same gorgeous colors which it was when we were on our way to Hull. Who can ever tire of looking at a grand sunset? Yet let me say here that when I was on the Sound steamer, on my way home to New London, Connecticut, I saw a more beautiful sunset than any I observed on the other side, the clouds being the most magnificent shades of red, purple and olive-green.

To go back to the North Sea, and to watching the sun go down. It would pass under a dark cloud and I would lose sight of it for awhile. Then the clouds would break, the edges being tinged with a gorgeous shade of red, and soon the sun would appear again in another place, looking as though it were bursting its way through.

Some of the party sat up until we reached Stavanger, on the Norwegian coast, and went on shore at 2 o'clock in the morning and took a ride about the city. All of us were up watching the lights along the coast till nearly

A Norway Fjord

midnight. The population of Stavanger is 25,000, and it is the oldest town in Norway, dating from the eighth or ninth century.

Next morning was clear and beautiful. We were passing the fjords and there on the shore here and there were trees and shrubs. Occasionally we saw little plateaus near the shore with a few houses on them. Someone said that the scenery reminded him of Alaska. Here were mountains with patches of snow on them, making them look very cold. Now we were passing the fjords and there on the shore were houses, plainly built, and here a pretty church. It was delightful to sit and watch the shore as we passed by, taking note of the queer homes of the people. In the distance were more snow-capped peaks; here was a light-house and a flag-station and there was a swing showing that the children were amused in about the same way all over the world. We saw near us eight little fishing boats, and farther on, not far from shore, pretty houses and trees, and once a manufactory. Here was a little field of grain growing (we had not seen one for some time) and high up on the slope of the mountain were cattle grazing. In a cosy, sheltered nook on the other side of the hill were some fishermen's houses and off there was a vessel anchored in the tiny harbor. Farther on was a light-house. And so the procession of sights passed by.

Just before reaching Bergen, opposite to the city as though to protect it, is a large fortification standing on top of a high mountain with mounted guns and men working upon it. As we approached Bergen we saw what appeared to be a little city nestled at the foot of a long chain of hills. It soon grew to be a large one, the most picturesque in its surroundings of any we saw in Norway.

The "Smeby Hotel" proved comfortable and wholly satisfactory. Mr. Smeby, Sr., had been to the World's Fair and liked to have a party of Americans stay with him. His son was the manager, and a jolly laugh and quick attention to the wants of his guests proved both his good heartedness and his efficiency.

At Bergen the courier whom the Manager had engaged to assist him upon the Continent appeared, and at once gained our kindly interest by his pleasant face and easy manners, and the knowledge he imparted to us that he had been wounded in the War of the Rebellion in America. Captain H. C. Nielson received his title, however, not in the army, but because he subsequently commanded a vessel which is at the bottom of the Atlantic. It seems that he came to America when about nineteen years of age to earn a livelihood, and soon after the war broke out enlisted. He was in the Grant campaign. At the close of the war he went to sea and repeatedly visited our country in Norwegian vessels. One which he commanded went down in a terrific storm off the coast of South America. He, with a few others, clung to the mast for a few days and were then taken off and saved, since which he has had no desire to continue life on the raging deep. He proved to be a competent interpreter and helpful guide.

In the afternoon we took a long drive and obtained an excellent idea of what Bergen, which was founded in 1070, is like. It is a beautiful city and a large one and the grand mountain scenery around it reminded me of Switzerland. The houses are built on a side hill, and I wonder they are not blown over in a heavy gale. High up above us one sees horses and carriages and that, too, reminded one of the way we travel in Switzerland. On our drive we went up the steep mountain side to see the old Viking mound and church, both about eight hundred years old, and the latter a curious specimen of architecture, reminding us of the pictures of the Chinese pagodas. Next to the capital, Bergen is the largest and most important town in Norway, having a population of 50,000. It is the center of the Norwegian fishing industry and fish export trade, as well as the principal station of the commercial steam fleet, and, owing to its many historical associations, it is generally considered to be one of the most interesting towns of northern Europe. It stands in the center of an amphitheater formed by seven surrounding mountains as we could see when we were on this delightful drive.

The dinner at Smeby's the first day was:

Soup.
Salmon, potatoes, cauliflower and caper sauce.
Chicken, potatoes, potato croquettes.
Cherries, plums and strawberries spiced.
Princess pudding with raspberry sauce.
Strawberries with sugar and cream.

And when we adjourned to the next room all were served with delicious coffee by a Norwegian maid in her peasant costume. On the edge of the bread plate at table was printed "Giv os I dag Vost Daglige Brod" (Give us this day our daily bread.)

After dinner the whole party went by electric tram to the cemetery to see the grave of

Ole Bull. We found the burial place, and a large urn in bronze marked the spot, with only "Ole Bull" engraved on the body of the urn, and on the standard "Died in 1880." The mound on which the urn stood was overgrown with ivy, roses and forget-me-nots. One of our ladies, who had heard Ole Bull play, laid a bouquet of wild flowers on his grave as a tribute to his memory.

Ten o'clock in the evening and we found we could write by the window in our room, and we had witnessed another magnificent sunset.

Next day was warm and delightful. We walked about the city, taking a peep into the stores where were all sorts of beautiful and curious things for sale—the furs and stuffed animals marvelously fine. We visited the markets and were charmed by their novelty. I must give our second day's dinner which consisted of:

Vegetable Soup.
Salmon trout with baked potatoes.
Boiled potatoes with chopped parsley and drawn butter.
Chicken; veal rolled in tomato and crumbs and fried with brown gravy.
Queen's pudding.
Strawberries with sugar and whipped cream.

Clearly Mr. Smeby does not allow his guests to starve.

On leaving Bergen we had a novel experience. We left the hotel, went down a flight of stone steps, entered a row-boat, crossed the harbor, ascended another flight of stone steps and there took the fine steamer "Neptun" for our trip up the fjords.

ELLEN COIT.

The Steamship "Neptun."

Lying by the dock at Bergen. This steamer makes various trips during the summer to the North Cape, but after August 1 goes only between Bergen and Trondhjem. It took the H. P. T. party on the latter voyage, a distance of 400 miles.

VI.

ALONG THE NORWEGIAN COAST.

WE left Bergen, Friday, July 23, 1897, about 11 P. M., favorably impressed with the city and with Smeby's Hotel, where we had been bountifully entertained. Boarding the good ship "Neptun" (Neptune) we steamed east of north along the coast of Norway, bound for Trondhjem, 398 miles. Looking at the map one would suppose our way would be chiefly through the open sea, but such is not the case. The course is principally through fjords and among islands, which for the most part constitute the western border of this country. Once during the entire route we were outside for about two hours, and again about an hour.

Our accommodations and meals on board were excellent; and these, with fine weather, beautiful scenery, stirring incidents and last, but not least, pleasant and congenial company, made the trip most delightful. The fjords and inlets, the islands and mainland present an almost endless variety of beauty and loveliness. Sometimes, too, a mist like a thin veil hung lightly over the valleys and again rose to the hill tops while we gazed in admiration. No description, however, can do justice to such scenery. The eye and heart alone can realize it.

For purposes of cultivation the contour of the land on either side improved northward; and on both sides, chiefly on the east, were small farm houses with a limited extent of tilled land attached. The crops were rye, barley, oats and potatoes. No wheat is raised so far north in either Norway or Sweden, and only a small quantity in the southern parts; and no maize in the two kingdoms. And just here, too, it may be stated that from the time the writer left New York, June 30, until he boarded the St. Paul at Southampton, September 4, he saw no Indian corn or meal in any form whatever, except a few plants grown for ornament in flower beds at railroad stations and elsewhere; and occasionally in Russia and Germany raised broadcast for fodder. On

A Norwegian Home

An early morning scene. The clouds are moving up the mountain, and the lady on horseback is about to assist as bridesmaid at a wedding in the country church, which is just visible in the background

the St. Paul we got both roasting ears and corn muffins.

The "Neptun" landed at Aalesund (population 8,000), and Christiansund (population 10,000) to put off and receive passengers and freight. Intermediate these cities lies Molde (population 1,800), a summer resort beautifully situated on an extensive and picturesque fjord. Here we arrived on Saturday afternoon and found at anchor the German Emperor's yacht, Hohenzollern, with His Majesty on board. We did not see him, but met officers and seamen of his vessel on the streets, having the name of the ship on their caps. The Hohenzollern is a beautiful model and was painted entirely white. The Emperor was making a pleasure cruise through the fjords with the German war cruiser Gefion acting as consort. The latter had already gone northward preceding the Hohenzollern, and we found her in the harbor at Trondhjem on our arrival there. She was also a model and painted white.

We visited a pretty church, seated upon an eminence in Molde, to see a celebrated picture, an altar-piece "The Resurrection," representing the angel sitting upon the vacant tomb, pointing heavenwards, and the women frightened and wondering. It is certainly artistic, lovely and touching.

From here also are seen the grand peaks of the Alps of the Romsdal and the towering top of the Romsdalhorn, higher than Vesuvius.

Proceeding on our route we passed fishing stations with moored boats and fishermen's huts, and reached Trondhjem on Sunday morning; and beside the Gefion found also here the American S. S. Ohio on her return from the North Cape with a large party. We gave them as we passed a hearty salute with our stars and stripes (which we carried everywhere) and received a similar greeting in return. We drove at once to the Britannia Hotel, and can give it a good name—commodious and well kept.

We attended divine services at the Cathedral, and though we did not understand a word of the ritual or sermon—the music, however, was excellent—we were deeply moved in worshipping with these earnest and devout people. The Cathedral is said to be the finest in the three Scandinavian kingdoms—Norway, Sweden and Denmark—and contains a replica of Thorwaldsen's great statue of Christ, presented by the artist himself.

The national church is Episcopal Lutheran,

Molde, Norway.

In the foreground is Molde, a fashionable summer resort, having a population of about 1,700. The large church visible contains the famous altar painting, "He is Risen," by Axel Ender. The water is the Molde Fjord, and beyond is the long chain of mountains known as the Romsdal, which vary in height from four to six thousand feet. The latitude of Molde is that of Frederichshaab, Greenland.

and almost the entire population of about 2,000,000 are members, a few thousand only being outside the fold.

Trondhjem is a flourishing city of about 25,000 inhabitants, in latitude 63° 26′ N., long. 10° 33′ E.; is modern in appearance, with wide streets and pavements, though having omnibus lines only—no street railways. It was founded, however, over 900 years ago by King Olaf Tryggvesson and then named Nidaros, being situated on the river Nid at its mouth. Here this king, known as Olaf I., set up and maintained a splendid court. The nation was then pagan, worshipping Odin and Thor, but Olaf had before his accession to the throne traveled extensively in Europe and England, and had imbibed Christianity, and had, moreover, married a sturdy and energetic English or Irish Christian woman; and at once with his whole power he set about the overthrow of paganism and the establishment of the Christian religion. He traversed the entire coast personally, destroying idols and baptising the prominent people. The measures employed were not always faultless as we now view things, but he and his two successors thoroughly accomplished their purpose, not only in this but also in cementing the divers provinces of Norway into a united and homogeneous kingdom with Trondhjem as its capital.

As all this occurred several centuries prior to the Reformation the new religion was, of course, Roman Catholic, and the Pope subsequently created here an Archiepiscopal See, making Trondhjem and its Cathedral the center and seat of power, and invested the Archbishop with authority over all Norway and its colonies, Iceland, the Orkneys and the Faroe islands. These Archbishops (successively) surrounded themselves with able and crafty officials, maintained great pomp and splendor, and gradually encroached not only on the rights of the people but also of the crown, almost ousting from power the Kings themselves. And so harrassing and exasperating did these encroachments finally become that the Reformation, when it came about, was gladly received and embraced by both King and people, and (not without struggles with the hierarchy), Lutheranism supplanted Romanism, and became and remains the national religion.

Both the spoken and written language is the Danish, with which kingdom Norway was connected, though independent, from about 1380 to 1814, A. D.

Along the Norwegian Coast.

Norway and Sweden though having the same King, the same representatives at foreign courts and same foreign policy are, in all other respects, wholly separate and independent. Each has its own constitution, legislature, laws, taxes, tariffs, coat of arms, flags, etc.; and all goods, merchandise, baggage, etc., passing from one country into the other are examined by custom officers and must pay the duties imposed.

Trondhjem continued for centuries the capital, and the Kings are still crowned in the Cathedral there as Kings of Norway, and the royal palace is maintained. The precise date of the founding of the city is not known, but it was A. D. 996 or 997, and the 900th anniversary of the event was celebrated there July 18, a week before our arrival, because that date happened to be an anniversary (24th) of the crowning there of the present King, Oscar II., and it also suited him to be present at that time. There is a growing party in Norway which advocates entire separation from Sweden under a new King, and they were preparing to celebrate the founding on July 29, three days after our departure.

The more we saw of the Norwegians the more we were persuaded that they are from the same stock as ourselves; are more like Americans than any other nation, even the English. Our preconceived impressions regarding Swedes and Norwegians were wholly reversed, the latter being the superior race. Throughout the country, too, we observed that their farm houses, barns, etc., are much better in every respect than in Sweden. The population indeed is chiefly rural, a very small per cent living in towns, and for the most part they own their farms and are not mere tenants. Schools are free and attendance, religious teaching and study of the English language obligatory. For generations also many of their young men have attended the German universities. So the diffusion of education has been general, and this with their religious training has implanted an independent intelligence and a stability and elevation of character which distinguishes them above the other races of Europe.

The climate of Trondhjem is good, being tempered and moderated by the sea, the wide and deep fjords and inlets, and the gulf stream on the coast. Its exports are chiefly salmon, cod, herring, oil and timber; and its imports textiles, hardware, groceries and American wheat and flour.

A Norwegian Stolkjærre.

The Manager and the Courier, with the "skyds-gut" (post-boy), in a stolkjærre at the inn near the Lerfos (waterfall), Trondhjem. This conveyance holds two persons; the more common one in use on postroads holds one only and is called a cariole. The latter is the more comfortable of the two. (*Photo. by L. A. Chase.*)

Of course we drove out to the celebrated Lerfos waterfalls—about five miles—and were delighted with their beauty and grandeur; and at the restaurant there we ate wild strawberries on July 26. The road was good, macadamed, and the scenery along the route fine. Some of our party were from Maine and they and others who had seen the Kennebec river united in pronouncing the two valleys exactly similar. On the roadside, at the foot of a small hill, stood a large guide board with this inscription in three languages, Danish, German and English, "Travelers are requested to walk up hill to spare the horses." We thought it unnecessary to comply. In this valley we saw new mown hay cured in a way quite new to us. A high fence of posts and rails or wire is built in the field and the hay is hung on the rails or wires, beginning at the bottom and continued to the top. Where there happens to be a fence along the roadside it is utilized in same manner.

Summing up some of the results of my observations during this delightful tour I conclude that Americans are better housed, clothed, fed and educated than any other people on earth. Nowhere are farm and country homes comparable with ours, nor anywhere else such an air of prosperity and happiness throughout the land. It has always seemed unaccountable to me how Europe could withdraw from work those immense armies and maintain and support these idlers and bear enormous burdens of taxation without collapse. The solution seems to be the severe and pinching economy everywhere practiced, and the fact that all the women and children are compelled to labor and often even the cows and dogs. In one field in Russia we saw fifteen women harvesting—some using sickles—and not a single man. Of course this was an extreme case. In regard to roads, however, we are greatly behind England and divers European countries, and to improvement in this respect our energies should be directed, assuring ample returns. In railroading we surpass every other country except only in passenger cars. The much criticized and condemned compartment coaches of England, Belgium and France are to my mind far more comfortable, separate yet sociable, and pleasant than our day, parlor and sleeping caravansaries. Neither is one annoyed and imperiled by smoke, cinders, dirt and blizzards inflicted through the raised window in front, or the often wide open doors both front and rear.

JOHN K. EWING.

VII.

ACROSS NORWAY.

OUR farewell to Trondhjem was indeed a memorable one, at least for a few of us. Our spirits, always buoyant, had led us to pilfer some signs which we spied hanging on our cars, and, not knowing the import of "optaget," we straightway begged our companions autographs. But our hilarity was soon tamed by the approaching gendarme, whose severe brusqueness quite took our breath away—likewise one of our cherished souvenirs; though we considered ourselves more than even when we, later, waved him a tantalizing "au revoir" with the remaining cards we had concealed under our jackets.

Though our journey was to be at night, we had no intention of sleeping, for here was our first and only opportunity of enjoying the interior scenery of Norway.

As we sped along we caught one last glimpse of the beautiful falls, the Lerfos, and passed on to the wilder country, where our first exclamation was caused by timber houses roofed with turf from which grew dwarf evergreen trees, sometimes to the number of a dozen. Quaint little stone churches were dotted here and there among the hills, and presently we found ourselves following the course of the beautiful Gula river, its waters so clear and green that the smallest pebbles were easily discernible.

Farther on our attention was attracted to a pretty rustic bridge, on the center of which stood a young peasant girl, perhaps another "Thelma," whose costume of red jacket and blue skirt added a picturesqueness to the scene never to be forgotten.

The fences were most curiously built of horizontal bars, through which were interwoven young saplings tied together with small twigs, and not standing upright, but all leaning toward the north, giving the effect of having been blown over by a windstorm.

At one of the stations were discovered two spears of corn planted as ornaments around a fountain, and it was amusing to see with what

King Oscar's Summer Chateau.

There are various summer residences on the islands and promontories in the Christiania fjords, but none so conspicuous or artistic as that of King Oscar II. It was built in 1849, is adorned with elegant paintings and stands in a beautifully wooded park   (*Photo. by M. Estil.*)

interest and joy we crowded around to inspect this little reminder of dear old America.

After passing through Roros, the highest point of our travels, a town situated on a bleak and dreary plateau where only the dwarf birch can thrive, we drew our curtains and prepared for a little rest before reaching Christiania.

We were not over-impressed with our introduction to Norway's capital, and were inclined to regret staying here two days, but a most charming sail arranged by our good Manager around the Christiania fjord, opened up to us its magnificent situation at the foot of pine-clad hillls; and our delight at seeing along its banks beautiful country homes, among them Oscarshall, the King's summer residence, also that of Nansen, the explorer, brought us back to the city in a more enthusiastic mood than when we started off on the little steam yacht "Turist."

As we sauntered up from the wharf, we wondered if Old Sol were not conspiring with Neptune to again entice us for a sail, for his rays were indeed unmercifully beating down upon our poor heads, and we gladly accepted an invitation to rest for a time at the House of Parliament or Storthings-Bygning, a handsome granite building, the façade flanked by two large stone lions. Our efforts in climbing the many flights of steps were rewarded by finding at the top the large room or "sal," where was being discussed by the members the question of narrow or wide-gauge tracks between Bergen and Christiania.

In the afternoon we visited the Winter Palace, and found it plain and unostentatious, a proof of the tastes and mode of living of King Oscar. Our interest was next divided between the two Viking ships, still in wonderful preservation, and some old church paintings hung on the walls of the sheds, the colors still marvelously bright, but the figures drawn with little idea of perspective or action.

Before returning to our hotel, I was greatly pleased to have pointed out to me the home of Dr. Henrik Ibsen, and later, at the Grand Hotel, I was again favored by having my café noir at a table adjoining that of this much talked of writer.

Great excitement was caused by the announcement on a news bulletin of the finding of Andree's balloon in one of the northern fjords, but later inquiries proved it to be a false rumor.

Some of our gentlemen took a carriole ride to Holmenkollen, and reported a remarkably

The Holmenkollen Hotel, Christiania.

This hotel is upon a mountain to the west of Christiania, 950 feet above sea-level. It commands a magnificent view of Christiania and the surrounding landscape, especially of the fjord. It is constructed of Norwegian pine, so treated that it has the appearance of mahogany. Both as to exterior and interior, it is believed to be one of the handsomest inns in the world.

beautiful hotel and extraordinary views of the fjord.

I must not leave Christiania without speaking of our delightful evening at the Tivoli gardens, of whose attractions we had been told by our kind friends who had visited them the evening before. And I think we all agreed that such dancing, tumbling and acrobatic performances could not be excelled even in renowned Paris, nor in our opinion could the great Sousa write a more inspiring march than was played for us "by request" that evening. That it was popular and "catchy" was proven by the many times heard refrain:

MABEL THERESE GUERIN.

VIII.

ACROSS SWEDEN.

HAS one, unfamiliar with this route, a mental vision of a narrow stream of muddy water, a tow path, a bony horse and a flat canal boat? If so, he must crowd that picture out of mind and become aware of the fact that our journey of two hundred and fifty or more miles and occupying two and one-half days is made through the river Göta Elf, and Sweden's three largest and most beautiful lakes as well as over canals of clear water, and upon a handsome steamer. Little lake Wiken, between lakes Wennern and Wettern, should also be mentioned on account of the beautiful effect produced by its tiny tree-covered islands, among which a course is marked out for the steamer to follow.

The canals are West Gotha, connecting lakes Wennern and Wiken; the East Gotha forming a water way between Wettern and Slätbaken, a long and narrow bay on the Baltic Sea, through which the steamer passes, and then sometimes skirting the shore and sometimes sailing in open sea it makes its way until at Södertelge it turns into a short canal connecting the sea with Lake Mälaren.

The locks through which the steamer passes in going from Gothenburg to Stockholm are seventy-four in number, fifty-six of them being used in the Gotha canals as a means by which the boats are enabled to rise to and descend from its highest point (300 feet) above the sea level. At Akersvass, near Trollhättan, where one may see the famous waterfalls, are the eleven locks constructed by Nils Ericsson, who in the years 1836-44 succeeded in the enterprise which the engineers Svedenborg and Polhem had undertaken in the early part of the eighteenth century and which they failed to accomplish because floating timber destroyed their work.

It may be interesting to take a look at the tiny steamer "Venus" which carried the Honeyman party of '97 on a most delightful journey through these canals and lakes. She is one hundred and seven feet long, and in width twenty-three and one-half feet according to Swedish measurement, which differs slightly from the English, a Swedish foot being a trifle the shorter. This little "Venus" is commanded by a Swedish captain who, assisted by one mate, gives orders to the six sailors. She will carry forty-one first-class and thirty-five third-class passengers and also freight. On the saloon deck are the dining-room, the captain's cabin and the "Konversation Salon." Forward in the stern and separated from the cabin deck by a slender railing, the third-class passengers assemble themselves.

As first-class travelers we were allowed the freedom of the boat. Such freedom was not to be despised and we all ascended many times the steep ladder-like stairway which led to the upper deck where the young and venturesome might (and did) sit on the covered life-boats and swing their feet, while more cautious pleasure seekers conversed with each other and the genial captain, who was always ready with a word—and more beside, in their own language, too—for his English-speaking passengers.

Below the saloon deck and reached by a staircase through the "Konversation" room are the state rooms—tiny ones, with space for two persons in each. One in the very stern of the steamer, called the saloon state room, has accommodations for six.

One member of the party seeing something that looked like an under deck passage to the stern of the steamer, and being curious in the matter of this boat's interior arrangement, followed the passage to the end and found herself under an open hatchway and close upon a small cargo of boxed cod fish. Her curiosity also turned her to the left and back through another narrow way at the end of which she found the cook and two maids in the kitchen. The visitor tried to open a conversation with the cook, but received only Swedish smiles in reply to questions. So, after satisfying herself that it was nothing unusual in the way of a kitchen, she answered with an American smile and left, ascending to the main deck to take one more look at Gothenburg.

The brown walled and serious looking building opposite the dock is the prison. After a glance at that the eyes travel back across the open square where the drivers gather with their carriages to the wharf, and there are quaintly dressed Swedish women who eagerly exchange gooseberries, cherries, apples and pears for öre, the small coin of the country, taking always as many as they can get.

It was at mid-day, on Friday, July 30, when the "Venus" left Gothenburg, one day later than had been planned because no trip was made on Thursday.

Perhaps through the endeavor to exchange English and American "coppers" for coin of the realm, a few members of the party had become acquainted with a banker of the city and his beautiful Russian greyhound. Anyhow, both dog and master drove to the wharf that Friday morning, just before the steamer's leaving time, to wish their American friends good-bye and a pleasant trip. Our eyes looked backward, as we glided away, at the banker on the wharf waving his most recent acquisition, an American flag. One patriotic young lady answered with her stars and stripes, and who shall say we left our first Swedish city without a farewell from friends?

So we were fairly started, and before the thorough enjoyment of the scenery began we were summoned to dinner in the little dining salon made to accommodate only twenty-four at one time. Our party, numbering twenty-six, filled the two tables pretty full. We were given the first sitting at all the meals, but even by this arrangement we were not enabled to breakfast until nine, dine at half-past

Street View in Gothenburg.

Gothenburg is one of the best-built and most attractive architecturally of the cities in Northern Europe. It is where the famous Gothenburg license system of dealing with the liquor problem is in force. It was founded in 1619, is located on a river, the Gota-Elf, about five miles from its mouth, and has numerous canals, one of which, in the Hamngatan, appears in the picture. Its population is about 115,000.

one and have supper served at half-past seven. In so doing, we gave up the dining-room to the native travelers in time for the very late meals customary in their country.

A slight delay in the service of our first meal was caused by our unfamiliarity with the Smörgasboard, or sandwich table. According to the Swedish custom, each one, as he enters the dining room, helps himself to a plate at the Smörgasboard, taking from there also small portions of the various relishes he may fancy— a sardine, a slice of tongue or cold meat, perhaps a quarter of a hard boiled egg, a taste of potato salad, or a piece of smoked salmon. Butter, if he wishes it, is almost always on the Smörgasboard. Having made his selection, he eats there, standing, and, later, takes his place at table. We, however, took to and ate at table these "appetizers;" after that the regular meal begins.

A very general stir in small quarters was the result when this custom was made known to us. The two pretty waitresses stood in the doors and watched the initiation of the Americans with interest. These maids, Pauline and Christine, Pauline especially, deserve more than a passing glance. Both were attired in the native costume, black velvet bodice outlined with gilt braid, worn over a white muslin guimpe and a short black skirt. Christine had a white apron, but it was Pauline who wore the pretty, bright striped one seen so much in Sweden. Pauline served coffee on deck to the Americans and when the native travelers desired refreshments it was she who brought the öl, a light beer, or the Swedish punch, which is a stronger beverage and very good—they so told us. Pauline knew a little English and when she wished us good night said "Sleep sweet." Pauline was—well any one might know it was an American who called Pauline a "peach."

But that first meal on board the "Venus" we shall not soon forget. There was soup, made very thick with carrots, peas and almost every other seasonable vegetable, which might have been called a vegetable compote quite appropriately. It was really good, which is more than may be said for the cherry soup, served to us two days later—a thick, oily substance, like a bisque with pitted cherries floating in it, a beautiful red in color and tasting like castor oil. We hoped that cherry soup would be well enjoyed at the second sitting and were quite willing to reserve our share, if thereby the Swedes might have a second portion. After soup we were given turbot, served with Hollandaise sauce and boiled potatoes; then boiled mutton accompanied by spiced currants and sliced cucumbers. Of bread, there were three varieties, white, rye and the Swedish knokkebröd, which is very coarse and dark and baked in round flat cakes about ten inches in diameter, like the Norwegian flad bröd, except that in Norway they mix caraway seed with the dough.

Our dessert, apple pie, had, it is true, an American name, but the similarity to our standby ended there. Well made apple pie is good, but the Swedish pie was worthy of even a better name. It was made with two crusts; between them and on top were layers of stewed apples; crowning this a thick layer of whipped cream dotted with bits of bright red jelly. The whole was cut in orthodox three-cornered pieces and served with a cold custard sauce. This pie found favor with the Americans, but custom did not stale it for us. Some one said there was a man from New Jersey who sought an interview with the cook and who, when he found that canal boat cuisine included such pie only once, wished that he had taken more than two pieces and—a photograph.

The after dinner coffee was served on deck

for twenty-five öre (6¾ cents) and with the coffee began our enjoyment of the unfolding panorama on each side.

Gothenburg is on the Göta Elf, and through that river we sailed for some hours, watching the tall grasses along the banks bend at our approach, the farmers mowing this same grass when not under water and the women doing their washing on flat stones or little wooden platforms built at the water's edge. We observed the washers as they spread the garments out and beat them with wooden paddles, and we felt sure that only clothing of the most durable texture could survive such treatment. On each side of the Göta Elf there is much rock of the gneiss formation and quantities of heather.

At Kungelf, a very old town on the left bank of the river, may be seen the ruins of what was once Bohusfort, built in 1308. This picturesque ruin stands on a rocky elevation and with its round tower and one window has the appearance of a savage Cyclops, always on guard.

Sailing on to Akerström we mounted, at that place, our first step in the staircase of locks. This one, named for Gustavus Adolphus, is the largest lock along the route. It was built in

1779 in order that the boats might pass a waterfall to be seen at the right. We watched the steamer's entrance with eager interest; the novelty of seeing the heavy sluice gates close behind us, after which those in front were slowly opened, gradually letting in the water upon which the steamer rose to a new level, never wore away throughout the trip.

As it required nearly two hours for the "Venus" to ascend the series of locks through which it rises to Trollhättan, there was ample time for those who wished to leave the boat at the first lock in this series, hire carriages and visit the falls, six in number. After a short drive from Åkersvass over a good road, we left the carriages and were guided through a pine grove to one of these waterfalls; imposing on account of the great volume of seething and foaming water, rather than the height of the falls, which is not great. From an iron carriage bridge built across the Trollhättan river, we were able to obtain a fine view of the Toppö fall; and near one end of this bridge we saw the old lock planned by Polhem nearly two hundred years ago but left unfinished.

We entered Lake Wennern in the evening, enjoyed a most beautiful sunset and spent all night in crossing that sheet of water.

Four masculine members of the party, desiring to see a Sunday in Stockholm, left the steamer Saturday morning, and hurried on by train. They missed much of the richest beauty of the canal; the fairest farm lands were passed that day and at times the canal narrowed to a silver thread, hardly more than the steamer's width, when branches of the trees on either side were within reach of the outstretched hand. Just at evening, near Vassbakken, we passed in a small grove of white birch trees on the right bank the brown stone shaft that marks the highest point on the canal. That four men should deliberately choose a dusty car ride in preference to the rural loveliness of this canal was incomprehensible; we sorrowed for them. And there were those of us who sent our sorrow forth in song, from the top of a life boat on the upper deck. Then was there American music in the Swedish air! And when the steamer halted at a little landing place the natives listened with manifest delight. There was a charm for the singers in the novelty of the situation and when a young woman called up from the wharf "Please sing the 'Bowery,'" we complied with a right good will and assured those Swedish people that we should "Never go there any more." The same

English-speaking admirer then asked for "Sweet Marie," and we sailed away, each one beseeching "Come to me!"

Sunday on the "Venus" was restful, and we observed that the native people were enjoying their day in a quiet though continental manner. Family groups and picnic parties in Sabbath day attire moved along the banks under the trees, sociably chatting together and eating their lunches they carried in peculiar, box-like baskets made of wood.

Sunday afternoon the steamer entered the Baltic and passed through a rain storm; the thought of its dreariness lent keener appreciation, a little later, as we began to enjoy the long lingering glory of the setting sun, which sent a radiant, golden pathway out athwart the sea.

During that short night we steamed close along the coast until the Södertelge Canal was reached. We passed through that and then across the eastern end of Lake Mälaren, arriving at Stockholm about four o'clock in the morning.

The "Venus" was our morning star and she held us, willing worshipers, until five o'clock, when Pauline served us with coffee and sweet cakes on deck. Then, almost under shadow of the historic Riddarholm Church, we waited for sleeping Stockholm to awake and give us welcome.

HENRIETTA F. WILLIAMS.

A Fjord View, About 9 P. M.

IX.

IN STOCKHOLM.

"IF you want to see the entrance to Stockholm you must be on deck before four o'clock to-morrow morning," said a friendly voice in my ear on Sunday evening, as I was going to my state room on the "Venus," which had been our home for nearly three days. It is an early start, I said to myself as I went below, but to miss that entrance of which I had heard such glowing accounts all my life was not to be thought of.

So, a little after three o'clock the next morning, found me on deck, watching the many green islands, more in number than the "Thousand Isles" of the St. Lawrence, with their pretty villas and gardens that make Lake Mälar so picturesque. As the "Venus" neared the wharf one after another of our party appeared on deck ready to welcome the sight of a new city with its picturesque surroundings. On our right the shores rise high above the water like a rocky parapet, and here, where a new road has lately been built winding in a zig-zag line to the top, enormous breweries have been erected and the commercial life of the city is evident. Large factories are also situated to the left, but here the shores are low and the impression is less striking.

It is, however, directly in front of the wharf that our attention is particularly directed, for here on the island called "The City" stand the two most interesting of the many stately buildings of Stockholm: Riddarholm, "The Westminster Abbey" of Sweden, and the Royal Palace where Oscar II. has his home. The church is finely situated in an open square in which is the figure in bronze of the founder of the city—the stern warrior King, who stands there in his armor of mail well pleased with the success of his creation. Within the church are buried the great and honored of Sweden's kings and warriors, Gustavus Adolphus, the great champion of the Lutheran Church in the North, Charles XI., the warlike but eccentric King, and Charles XIV., or Bernadotte, the founder of the present dynasty. Some famous

Generals of the Thirty Years' War also rest here, while the armorial bearings of many royal homes draw strongly upon one's historical knowledge. Aside from the association thus aroused there is little in the church itself to excite attention, and perhaps the most interesting thought that lingers in my mind is that of a faded wreath hung on the outside wall, which on the anniversary of the death of the King is every year renewed. My companion, a sweet Swedish woman with whom I took my first walk in Stockholm that Monday morning, while waiting for the hotel to open, pointed to the wreath and told its history, adding: "No one knows who the woman is that brings it, but she never fails to hang a fresh one there each year."

This Swedish lady was ever ready with true northern courtesy to render any aid in her power to us as tourists from the far-away New World, and I am sure many of us will long remember her slight figure, sweet face and gentle smile as she stood on the deck of the "Venus," quick to translate into English a puzzling sentence or explain some bewildering custom.

Among the pleasantest of the many pleasant memories of travel are those faces, which, from time to time, recur to us as belonging to some who by word or deed have made a foreign city seem less strange and more like home. I recall at this moment the voice and face of a young man who in a store in Stockholm stepped forward and in excellent English arranged a desired purchase for me, and on being questioned with regard to his English answered that he had been eight years in a picture store in Providence, R. I.; a store, by the way, well known to me in my occasional visits to that city. Truly the world is small, we say, in thinking of these things.

All I had ever been told of Swedish courtesy was more than realized in Stockholm; for it was here that coming out of the Exposition grounds with one of our party we found ourselves in an unknown part of the city and could see no cab nor tram-car at hand. We accosted with all the languages at our command several persons, receiving only anxious, uncomprehending looks, until a lady rose from a seat in a park near by and coming toward us, in exquisite French and an exquisite manner, sent us rejoicing on our way. Her face is as vividly before me now as are many of the fine portraits in the art gallery of the Exposition; for the great attraction of Stockholm this year is the Exposition.

The Exposition was held in the new buildings erected near and in the Djurgärden or Deer Park. The exhibition was most interesting, but the collection of pictures by the best artists of Scandinavia chiefly attracted me. To many Americans the exhibit at the World's Fair in Chicago of these northern artists was a revelation of color and technique. Here at Stockholm was an opportunity to see on a larger scale the work of the Swedish, Norwegian and Danish artists. Zorn, Oscar Björck, Carl Larsson and Prince Eugene were well represented by characteristic works. These all belong to the Impressionist School, but their coloring is more brilliant than that of the more southern schools. But this very brilliancy of coloring, which had perplexed me in America as I studied their paintings, was now easily comprehended after seeing the wonderful sunrise and sunset effects in these northern lands. These Swedish and Norwegian painters have a right to their rich colors which are not mixed with imagination but with realism. The brilliant reds which Zorn so well knows how to use, as, for example, in the portrait in the Stockholm Exposition of a young girl standing ready as it were to spring from the canvas and extend a hand of welcome to the stranger before her, are here subdued but without losing their vividness by the rich brown of the fur thrown over one shoulder, while the whole impression is as weird as are some of the effects of light and shade in this land of the midnight sun.

Björck is a painter who does not perhaps produce as startling effects as Zorn, for he seems to hold his power in reserve and by this very self-control he attracts and holds the attention. A half-length portrait of the young "Fru E," at the Exposition is one of his most fascinating pictures. Amused at something she has heard, or somebody she has seen, perhaps yourself as you stand before her, she looks out from the canvas with a bright smile of recognition on her face, while you stop involuntarily to catch, if possible, the explanation from her parted lips. A fair young woman she is in her light blue dress, with only the delicate lace tracery of a screen behind her and the simplicity of the work is as striking as the fiery ardor of Zorn's creation in her red dress and girlish mirth. The pictures seem typical of the two painters, and may account for the preference which the Swedes themselves give to Björck over his brother artist.

The study of these northern pictures on a

The King's Garden, Stockholm.

This view of the "Kungstradgard" is in the heart of Stockholm. It is open to the public, and is adorned with fountains, statues, and is surrounded by some of the most tasteful modern buildings in the city. The Royal Palace appears in the background, to the right of centre.

showery afternoon, when the brilliant sunlight and the dark rain clouds strangely alternated without, left an indelible impression on my mind and a firm conviction that Scandinavian art has a great part yet to play in the artistic life of the world.

One of the charms of Stockholm is that excursions are easily made by tramway or boat to all the environs of the city. A few of our party had a delightful trip given by the Manager on one of the little steamers to Drottningholm, the summer residence of the King. The pretty villas on the island and mainland as we passed looked invitingly at us, but we were eager to see the Palace, and I think hardly appreciated their beauty and simplicity. Yet Drottningholm itself is refreshingly simple; a country home where life can be spent apart from the ceremony that is the usual accompaniment of royalty. Many interesting pictures by Scandinavian artists of the old school, (which was that of Dusseldorf), and some by foreign painters adorned the walls, and in the large ball room was an interesting gallery of portraits of all the sovereigns of Europe who were cotemporary with Oscar I., the father of the present King. Exquisite models of Greek and Roman statues and architecture were scattered through the apartments as if the collector, probably Oscar I., who did much to beautify the place, had taken a real pleasure in bringing them together.

On one side the grounds of Drottningholm reach to the waters of the fjord and on the other side the garden, stretching away into the distance, reminds one, as indeed do all royal gardens, of Versailles.

Stockholm is well supplied with horse-cars, though the method of taking the fares of the passengers seems to an American very primitive. The conductor carries in his hand what seems at first sight to be a small lantern, but further inspection proves to be a receptacle into which, by means of a slit in the top, the passengers can drop his 10 öre, or three cents, the price of his ride.

If the Swedes in this case still cling to an old custom, they have at least adopted some new ones, as for instance the telephone, which it is said is more freely used in Stockholm than in any other city of the world.

As we entered Stockholm from the west in the early morning, it was fitting that our departure should be from the east and just before sunset. We were starting for Russia on one of the fine steamers that ply between Stockholm and St. Petersburg, but even that fascinating country could not dampen our ardor for the pleasure we had found in the sister kingdom of Norway and Sweden; and the remembrance of our delightful visit to Stockholm, with its courteous people, its well-beloved sovereign and its fascinating position, will ever be one of the choicest recollections of our almost faultless summer wanderings of 1897.

CHARLOTTE TITCOMB.

X.

FINLAND AND ST. PETERSBURG.

AS our pretty little steamer, the "Tornea," the best we had found in Northern European waters, drew up gently to the wharf at Helsingfors, the capital of Finland, it found us all eagerly waiting to land, for our intense desire now was to enter one of the funny carriages in waiting and explore the city. At last our wish was gratified; eleven droskies, each containing two persons, started. The night came down all too soon and we had seen little; so we finished the remaining few hours of our stay at the Public Garden, where two bands were playing, the one composed of women, who played remarkably well. Of course, owing to our hurried trip, I could hardly write at great length of Helsingfors, but I was impressed most favorably with its location and beautiful harbor.

At 1 A. M. we were en route for St. Petersburg. For many years my most ardent desire had been to visit Russia. The book of George Kennan, the lectures of John L. Stoddard and the numerous accounts given of that wonderful and mysterious country had only served to increase that desire to see all those glories for myself; and so, when the steamer approached the low-lying shores off Cronstadt, I experienced that thrill of nervous anticipation only felt when one is about to visit an unknown land; visions of all I had ever read or heard of detentions, imprisonments, police surveillance and other like experiences, passed before my mental vision, especially as I saw a dozen or more huge Russian war vessels waiting to receive the Emperor of Germany, due the next day.

At St. Petersburg I put on a bold front and passed with my fellow-travelers to the wharf. As anticipated, a demand was made for "passports" by an officer stationed at the gangplank. I calmly informed him in plain English that "our courier attended to those matters," and, while he was struggling with astonishment, started forward, and, under the guidance of the colored porter of our prospective hotel, entered one of the carriages in waiting. After a delay of one hour, we were allowed to depart.

During a sojourn of several days in St. Petersburg, we found that the great secret of success in surmounting all difficulties was to ignore completely those who spoke Russian to us and follow our own sweet will, for, either tiring of our imperturbability, or else thinking our silence characteristic of Americans, they invariably shrugged their shoulders and retired. The city presented a most beautiful appearance, in gala attire, in honor of the visit of Emperor William to the Czar. Flags floated from every building, columns were wound with the imperial colors, red trimmed with ermine, or rather white canton flannel, dotted with small pieces of black cloth. Even with this holiday aspect, I was at once struck with the hopelessness of life in Russia. There was seemingly no mirth. I rarely heard a laugh and in the streets there was such an absence of conversation. Every one moved along in a half-hearted fashion, in marked contrast to the Paris and London which we had so recently left.

One evening, in the salon, a young officer was seated near one of our party. Entering into conversation with him, the officer pro-

Russian Drosky and Driver.

The universal cab of Russia. It usually has rubber tires in Finland and St. Petersburg, and is exceedingly comfortable. The horses are driven at great speed. The driver's gown is blue, reaching to his feet, and is gathered about the waist, giving him a portly look. His hat is not the most handsome ever invented.

posed that the party should visit Peterhof, one of the summer residences of the Imperial family and just then en fête, and said he would take particular pleasure in showing us its beauties. Of course, we availed ourselves of his unlooked-for invitation, and it was owing to his courteousness and excessive kindness that we were enabled to view Peterhof's charming and novel attractions.

How can I describe the fairy-like scene we witnessed there? Our drive was through the large park, with its innumerable fountains all playing, without limit to their number and variety. Numberless mythological subjects figure in these fountains, and I recall one particularly, the fountain of Samson, where Samson is contending with a lion, which throws up a jet of water to the height of eighty feet. We saw an artificial tree, each leaf and twig sending forth a stream of water. In one pond are fish that will come to be fed at sound of a bell. As our time was limited, we contented ourselves in gazing where these fish were supposed to be.

I read recently an incident told of Prince Bismarck, when he was the Prussian ambassador at the Czar's Court, and which admirably illustrates Russian absolutism. He was standing one day at a window of the Peterhof palace with Alexander II., when he observed a sentinel in the center of a spacious lawn with apparently nothing whatever to guard. Out of curiosity he inquired of the Emperor why the man was stationed there. Alexander turned to an aide-de-camp, "Count Schonfalof, why is that soldier stationed there?" "I do not know, your Imperial Majesty." The Czar frowned and answered curtly: "Send me the officer in command for the day." Presently the officer appeared, pale with apprehension. "Prince Ivanovitch Poniatowsky, why is a sentinel stationed on that lawn?" "Really, your Majesty, I—I do not know," stammered the officer. "Not know?" cried the Czar in surprise. "Request then the general in command of the troops at Peterhof to present himself immediately." A few moments later the commandant hurried to the spot in a state of great fear and agitation. "General Petrovitch Sscherneschewski Bogoljnbof Nijninovgorodinski," asked the Czar, "will you be kind enough to inform us why that soldier is stationed in yonder isolated place?" "I beg to inform your Majesty that it is in accordance with an ancient custom," replied the general evasively. "What was the origin of the custom?" calmly inquired Bismarck. "I—I do not at present recollect," stammered the officer. "Investigate the subject and report the result," the Czar said. The investigation began and, after three days and nights of labor, it was ascertained that about eighty years before, one morning in spring, Catherine II. observed in the center of this lawn the first mayflower of the season lifting its delicate head above the lately frozen soil. She ordered a soldier to stand there to prevent its being plucked. The order was duly inscribed upon the books; and thus for eighty years, summer and winter, a sentinel had stood upon that spot, no one, until Prince Bismarck's time, caring to question the reason of the custom.

Leaving Peterhof we returned to St. Petersburg to prepare for our little trip to Krasnoe-Selo, the great military camp, where the review of troops by the Emperor William was to take place next day. The box and seats the members of our party occupied were in front of the grandstand, and on the vast plain in front of us was drawn up regiment after regiment, awaiting the arrival of the two Emperors. In the distance we heard a muffled sound, which, becoming more distinct, heralded the approach of those we had been so anxiously awaiting. On horseback came the two upon whom all eyes were riveted, the Emperor riding on the right of the Czar; in an open carriage came the two Empresses, bowing to the shouting multitude. The band of one thousand pieces played, and we saw royalty and its full court in court dress. Later, a few special ones with the crowned heads passed into a tent prepared for them, and, after some feasting, the Emperors and Empresses entered a carriage and were driven down the road directly in front of us. For the time being we were as patriotic Russians as those about us, and when the Emperors saluted the little American flag which one of our party waved, we felt that our day had been a most successful one.

It was then nine P. M. and the forty bands struck up the evening prayer; it was responded to in singing by the different regiments, and as the beautiful strains grew fainter and fainter in the distance, we turned our faces homeward, sorry that the brilliant pageant was over. Hurrying to the cars we were literally lifted into a third class compartment, by the struggling crowd, but as the occupants were pleasantly disposed Russians, we concluded to remain rather than try our luck elsewhere.

Of the hair-breadth escapes while driving on

the Nevski Prospect, only those who have had a like experience can testify. In Russia the horse seems to be in full accord with his master, but during my first drive I clutched the side of the drosky to keep from being precipitated on the cobble stones. After a few turns around corners, however, seeing that we kept our equilibrium, it became quite exhilarating.

The drosky drivers are a stolid set of men, never seemingly moved by anything, excepting the occasional thumps we gave them to indicate that we wished to stop or move on; for after a glance at the Russian alphabet, I did not have the ambition to even learn yes or no.

One funny experience was, when wishing to go from a certain church to our hotel, we signaled a drosky, mentioning the hotel to the driver. He shook his head. With the determination of Americans we jumped into the carriage and motioned him to go on. The first corner we gave him a thump and waved to the right; next corner another thump and a wave to the left; and so on, until we reached the hotel. After paying him his fare, I stood on the carriage step and said three times slowly: Hotel d'Angleterre!" making him repeat it after me. That lesson in English was given for the benefit of future visitors to St. Petersburg. A smile illumined his features and we parted most amicably, notwithstanding the numerous thumps in his side. I trust he profited by his lesson.

Sunday morning was devoted to visiting the different churches, chiefly the Kazan Cathedral, with its wealth of treasure, and St. Isaac's, with its magnificent dome covered with gold and surrounded by thirty monolithic shafts. Owing to the kindness of a soldier on guard we were allowed to go up nearly to the altar of St. Isaac's during service. The musical, sonorous voice of the priest, who intoned the service; the deep devotion of the kneeling multitude; the light on the ornamentations of jasper, porphyry, and malachite, all made up a whole so exquisite as to seem scarcely real.

On Monday, our last day in St. Petersburg, we visited the Winter Palace, the most beautiful I have ever seen (with the exception of the one at Moscow). It contained room after room of matchless beauty, with polished floors, crystal chandeliers, and exquisite souvenirs, filled with the memories of those who had peopled them at different times and who had so often met with an untimely death. The

The Singing Deacon of St. Isaac's.

An accurate likeness of the chief intoner of the Greek Church litany in St. Isaac's Cathedral, St. Petersburg ; the man whom all visitors to that cathedral remember as having a voice like one of the great bells in the tower ; or, as one writer says, "whose basso profundo, of incredible power, resounds like the notes of a great organ to the remotest end of the building."

Romanoffs have been an unfortunate race, rarely living to a serene old age.

As I left St. Petersburg, on our way to Moscow, and saw her disappear in the gathering twilight, I felt that it had been a joy to have seen her.

ABBIE RANLETT MASON.

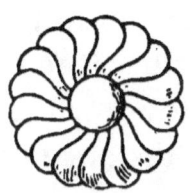

XI.

THE OLD RUSSIAN CAPITAL.

MOSCOW, the golden, Moscow, the magnificent, we have seen thee, greeted thee, and are quite willing to bid thee good-bye.

Our expectations were overweening or our pride would not have had so sudden a fall. We really expected an oriental city of dazzling splendor at the first outlook from our railway window, and we discerned, instead, simply coarsely-painted, low, white buildings, with enough dust in the distance to warrant our belief that we were coming to a Sahara. We looked for mosques; we saw only wretched buildings, a plain and poor station, and a motley crowd of disagreeable looking people.

We had left St. Petersburg at seven P. M. and traveled all night in pretty comfortable sleeping coaches, at a pace of nearly forty miles an hour. That railway we knew to be in almost a straight line, for did not an emperor lay his ruler upon a map and indicate that it must run that course, regardless of cities, or streams, or desert? So far as we knew, we swung around no curves and climbed no mountains. When morning came we had a good breakfast in a dining car and then looked out upon a rather sterile, flat country, with villages that seemed to be composed only of small, unpainted barns, with zigzag roadpaths running hither and yon regardless of a surveyor's draught, and with little else of interest. There were white birches, and straggling forests, and occasionally a harvest field. Before we seemed aware of it, when the hour said half-past nine, we arrived at our destination.

If we could have come at once in view of the kingly Kremlin, entered its antique portals, climbed the Ivan Tower, and looked out upon the magical scene there presented, we should— I am sure I should—have thanked God that we were permitted to gaze even for a moment upon such Byzantine splendors. But it was not to be. We went down through despair to reach the heights later. We bowed low in the dust and grime, saw wretchedness and want, and then our souls grew faint and some one cried aloud, "Take, oh take us quickly away from this Russia; we hate it, we loathe it; it is intolerable."

I confess now to a timorous apprehension during some weeks before that our Moscow days might be those of disappointment. The feeling increased at St. Petersburg, and grew apace as we neared the storied capital. And now that we were there, should we see only dirt and poverty, and candidates for Siberian emigration? Some would have left the city forthwith, shaking the dust from our feet and departing with speed. But it was too much to agree to leave for Warsaw before we had even tried to hunt up the Kremlin, and so I could not promptly join my fellow-Egyptians in their murmurs.

Our hotel was not as sweet and clean as the Waldorf, though it was fairly good. It was the "Berlin," kept by a Swiss gentleman, who spoke English well, German perfectly, and Russian perhaps worst of all. He was attentive to our wants, enlightened our minds plentifully on the subject of the taxes of Russia, and how it was that his hotel was (in his view) economical to travelers above other hotels. I think he really meant to make us comfortable and happy, but we were not very willing to be so.

I might as well jot it down now that in Russia we were not exactly afraid of Siberia or the passport examiner, but we were just a mite uncomfortable from day to day. Those passports had to be viséd so frequently. There was such an embargo placed on inter-communication because of the outlandish language the people spoke and their stubbornness in not understanding English. The drosky drivers were such barbarians in conduct and gesture. There was so much of the Tartar in the street walkers and so little of the Christian in the street sights, notwithstanding the shrines of saints at every corner, that some grew afraid. I judge Moscow, like St. Petersburg, to be entirely safe to man or woman at any hour of the day and up till the night's zenith, but we lacked faith!

Moscow was dirty and hot, and altogether disagreeable in its cobblestone pavements—the worst, by the way, I ever saw in any city. If Zion is a hard hill to climb, harder is the path up to and around the Kremlin, the altar of Moscow and the glory of Russia.

That Kremlin, when we once saw it from

the Ivan height, was simply superb in its splendors. No one then thought of hovels or barbarians, but of the magnificent prodigality of brain that devised, and the tremendous strength of will that executed such minarets, domes and cathedrals, such palaces, monasteries and treasure houses.

To understand the relation of the Kremlin to present Moscow, you must conceive of a city on a plain, of 850,000 inhabitants, and in its center a slight, square hill, and on that hill pile up all the architecture of Tartar khans and Romanoff princes and Czars, from Dolgoronski, in 1147, to this day; a heterogeneous, but wonderfully rich mass of color and picturesqueness, and you have the Kremlin. It is within stone walls, perhaps twenty feet high, pierced with five gates, and to-day contains treasures never exceeded by Solomon's Temple.

To comprehend why Moscow is what it is one must recollect that in the reign of Ivan I., about five hundred and sixty years ago, Moscow was the supreme city of the three competing for supremacy within ancient Russian territory. It held that position until 1812, when its inhabitants gave up overmuch of their proud possessions to the devouring element, preferring to burn down their homes and melt up their jewels, and so rob Moscow of all its glory, rather than yield to the ambition of Napoleon. It was one of the grandest sacrifices ever made upon a national altar of flame and sword. Happily there is enough left to astonish visitors now as did the wonders of the East that famous traveler, Marco Polo.

The imperial residence was transferred to St. Petersburg in 1711, in the time of Peter the Great, but the latter city made no pretensions to equal the goodly wealth of decoration of the more ancient city. Petersburg's inhabitants number 1,200,000; Moscow's, 850,000; but, notwithstanding the self-immolation of 1812, the wealth piled up against the columns and upon the altars of the cathedrals and in the other public buildings of Moscow probably outrival that of any city in Europe.

There are two ways of securing a just impression of the magnificence, as to its gold and jewels, of this old Tartar heritage. The first, which is the way in which a stranger should early secure the impression, is to climb by easy steps what is known as the Ivan Tower, and then, at the height of something less than three hundred feet, when beneath the gilded cupola, survey the Kremlin at his feet. Going up this Ivan Tower, by the way, you will pass by a large number of bells of various sizes and tones, perhaps as many as fifty. The largest weighs sixty-four tons. The smaller are two silver bells, said to be exquisite in tone and of beautiful contour. It is the ringing of all these bells on Easter eve which produces a memorable effect upon visitors.

From this elevation one sees below him, within a stone's throw, gold-crowned cathedrals, monasteries, the Arsenal, the Royal Palace, and beyond them, walls; then the Moscow river, great squares, towers and mosques of all colors, and beyond these other cathedrals with domes dipped into the rainbow and burnished by the sunlight into opulent iridescence.

The next natural method to deepen the impression of the richness of these architectural splendors, is, after descending, to enter each of the more prominent buildings near the tower and within the Kremlin walls.

There is, for instance, the Cathedral of the Assumption, in which all the Russian Emperors are crowned. Its five domes are resplendent with gold over copper, and its pavement is of jasper and agate. Within there are jeweled icons, shrines covered with diamonds and em-

Cathedral of the Assumption, Moscow.

The venerable church in which the emperors have been crowned from Ivan II. (1353) until now. It is a mixture of Byzantine and Lombard types of architecture, dates from 1326, and contains the tombs of the founder, St. Peter, first Metropolitan of Moscow, and other Patriarchs. Each of its five domes is covered with gold and its wealth of gold and jewel ornamentations and of sacred pictures in the interior is almost incalculable.

eralds, pillars of pure gold, frescoes thoroughly Byzantine, marbles from Sienna, and porphyry from Finland. And to the worshipers it is a place of peculiar veneration, because of the coronation ceremonies which have been held within its walls since the time of the Russian patriarchs. Here are buried all those early metropolitans of Moscow, beginning with St. Peter, who built the first church on the spot in 1326 and the primates of the church; and here are single pictures adorned with jewels to the value of more than $200,000 each. One can neither enter nor leave this wonderful sanctuary without being surprised at its smallness considering its historical associations, nor without being overwhelmed at a sense of the magnitude of the offerings of those wicked men and pious women, who, in former days, through motives of so-called religion, gave almost all that they possessed to adorn this temple.

Then, very near by, is the Cathedral of the Archangel Michael, another building with five gilded domes, over six hundred and fifty years old in some portions, and all of it over four hundred and eighty years of age; the mausoleum of two of the most ancient dynasties of the Czars. Herein lie Ivan, the Terrible, and his assassinated son, and about the latter's tomb are various personal relics, including his own portrait in frame of finest gold. This church contains one of the earliest copies of the Gospels known in Russia, a treasure house, and icons not less remarkable than in the Cathedral of the Assumption, and the whole effect of the interior is that of a duplicate of the last named. It constitutes but one more "embarrassment du richesse."

The monastery close at hand is almost as wonderful; a temple of gold and silver. But we specially admired the Treasury House in the right wing of the palace. Here are deposited the venerable historical objects of the reigning house of Russia; the royal plate, the pearls, the diamonds, the rubies; all the thrones of the former and present emperors and empresses; their coronation robes, the royal carriages, the crowns. One crown alone, the gift of the Shah of Persia in 1604, contains 2,200 rubies and pearls. I saw here an orb which, if it ever had any use, must have been chiefly to prove the reckless prodigality of the old Romanoff princes, for it was studded with 58 diamonds, 89 rubies, 23 sapphires, 50 emeralds, and 37 pearls! And, in another crown, used by the Empress Anne, but originally made for

Catherine I., by order of Peter the Great, the diamonds in it numbered 2,536! And vases of vermeil, tables of silver, placques of other precious metals and similar articles, innumerable, incalculable in value, of no use save to look at, are in this Treasury House.

From here one passes around to and enters the Palace proper, to describe which in the space allotted me would be impossible. There are three halls in the Palace, either one of which would seem to put to blush even that exceedingly beautiful hall in the Winter Palace at St. Petersburg, known as the Nicholas ballroom. They are, first, the Hall of St. George, two hundred feet long and of proportionate width, the rooms all in gold and white, with exquisite hardwood floors and walls inscribed in gold with the thousands of names of the members of the order. It has crystal chandeliers holding 3,200 candles. The next is the Alexander Hall, only half as long, but lighted by 4,500 candles; a room in pink and gold, filled with gorgeous paintings. The third is the Hall of St. Andrew, fluted like a Gothic cathedral, whose walls are gold and pale blue, and at whose end are two thrones of the Emperor and Empress, the steps to which are covered with a carpet of cloth of gold. This Palace is only fifty years old and its present use may be guessed at rather than understood.

At the foot of the Ivan Tower lies what is known as the Great Bell of Moscow, otherwise called the "King of Bells," which was cast in 1733 from an older bell of 1654, which itself was cast from a bell of 1633, which was perhaps itself a child of the bell of 1553, the first large Russian bell of which we have any record. Its weight is about 400,000 tons. It stands more than twenty-six feet high, and is over twenty-two feet in diameter, with a broken piece, seven feet high and weighing eleven tons, along its side. The tradition is that the ladies of Moscow threw into the liquid metal so many jewels and other treasures that there was an imperfection in the last casting, but whether from this reason or from the falling of heavy rafters in a fire in 1737, it is certain that soon after it was cast it fell to the ground and was quite buried out of sight for almost a century. In 1836 Nicholas I. lifted it upon a pedestal, and there it stands as one of the wonders of the world.

I can but allude to some of the 450 other churches outside the Kremlin. There is the cathedral of St. Basil, whose exterior is half barbaric, like a Hindoo pagoda, full of cupolas

Cathedral of St. Basil, Moscow.

Built to commemorate the "prophet and worker of miracles," St. Basil, (also known as the "patron of idiots"), who was buried on this spot, A.D. 1552. Three years later this edifice was begun, the architect being an Italian, who, tradition says, had his eyes put out by order of Ivan IV., "in order that he should not build another edifice like it." In both exterior and interior architecture it is one of the most curious structures in Russia. The colors of its domes are as numerous as those of the rainbow.

carved to the resemblance of pineapples, melons, artichokes and other odd designs, and colored with the several colors of the rainbow. It is as beautiful as a dream and as crazy as its patron saint. Directly in front of the St. Basil, as if to give plenty of space to a spot whose associations must be forever hideous, is the Red Square, once a veritable field of blood. Here is the circular stone from which the iron edicts of the Czars were proclaimed and here were the eighteen gibbets erected by Ivan when he kept his instruments of torture at deadly work. Here Peter the Great beheaded the Streltsi conspirators. The square has two redeeming features aside from the cathedral—the New Bazaar, to be spoken of hereafter, and the Redeemer Gate to the Kremlin, architecturally graceful, and upon which is the picture of Christ, known as the "Redeemer of Smolensk," before which every head, even that of the Czar himself, must uncover, if its possessor is to pass beneath the portal. The "pious" Russians kiss the pavement beneath it; we honored their custom by removing our hats.

Probably the most wonderful object architecturally, at least as viewed from a distance, is the Church of the Saviour, built to commemorate the deliverance of Moscow from the

French invasion. It is of white stone, with four belfrys, each surmounted by a golden cupola, and over the whole rises an immense gilt dome. The building is large enough to hold 7,000 persons and up to the highest parts it attains the height of three hundred and fifty feet. I did not get to it nor enter it, an omission I now regret. Nor did any of us, I think, enter the picture galleries or museums of the city, all of which were modern, but immense in size, and of most interesting architecture.

A still greater loss than these, however, was our inability to visit and to study the battlemented walls and the interior, six-domed churches of the Novo Devitchi Convent, whose perspective was so attractive when viewed from Sparrow Hill. As a mere harmony of architectural colors, it was bewitching, and I am told the red bell-towers and green roofs, yellow crosses, and light blue frescoes were not mere colors, but actual artistic achievements. Perhaps it was as well we did not get nearer, for, beside the beautiful buildings, we should have had pointed out to us the house of sad Sophia, Peter the Great's sister, who, while imprisoned there, looked out from her window upon the hanging in cold blood of the two hundred conspirators, who were first tortured and then swung up, because they had the bad judgment to oppose tyranny and sigh for liberty. Surely all the marvelous gorgeousness of the Novo Devitchi cannot save its associations with the history of unjudicial murders.

We saw in Moscow some of the dirtiest and most repulsive of the Russians, who, were they Tartars or otherwise, deepened our conviction that to keep such in repression required a strong government; an ordinary form of monarchy would scarcely subserve the interests of public order in Russia. And, strange to say, we saw some of the same greasy-looking beggars, whose feet were in burlap, with unkempt head and dress, and packs upon their backs, shown through the Treasury House in the palace with almost the same courtesy that was extended to visitors of intelligence and culture. They had simply to leave their packs at the door and were ushered by officials before the elegant thrones and through the sumptuous halls as if they had been millionaires.

Moscow shops had enormous signs, none of them containing a word which we had ever seen before. There was the big New Bazaar, the finest externally and the largest in dimensions within I ever remember to have seen, covering, perhaps, four ordinary American city blocks; a white building of stone, three stories high, where everything (but what you desire) is sold. The markets contained provisions not at all dear; but living is high in Russia because of the enormous taxes and correspondingly enormous rents. The Tartar drivers of droskies seemed to be distinguishable by feathers in their hats, but I judge the majority of that wild clan were to be found among the commoner laborers who drove the brick wagons, which usually line the streets and which come in from the country. On one of the streets we saw scores, if not hundreds, of such wagons, proving that building operations in Moscow are as extensive as elsewhere.

And now, lastly, as to the one trip we took away from the Kremlin. We shall always remember it in connection with this city—the drive out to Sparrow Hill. That is an eminence some two miles or more beyond the tower-crested rim of the city, to the west, and is the spot from which Napoleon first had sight of the fevered mirage of his soul—Moscow. It was from that hill he attained, or within twenty-four hours afterward, the summit of his ambition, and from it, on his retreat,

The King of Bells, Moscow.

Cast in 1733, under Empress Anne, but fell down in four years' time, and, ninety-nine years later, (1836) Nicholas I had it erected on a pedestal, beside the Ivan Tower, where it now stands. Total weight about 400,000 pounds; weight of the broken piece about 22,000 pounds.

(*Photo. by M. Estil.*)

heard the echoes of his downfall. To reach this spot, we drove over about four miles of the cobblestone pavement, which, let me again repeat it, is the worst on earth. Succeeding it, while in a totally exhausted condition from the noise and shake-up, we encountered a stretch of dust three inches deep. As our carriages followed each other closely, we simply "choked to death," and only had resurrection when Sparrow Hill was announced. That ride was something so dreadful upon nerves and lungs that it required superhuman courage to resolve to return at all to the capital, or to our hotel. We felt it in our bones, spine, hips, feet, head, and I cannot wonder that no person of our brave twenty-five had courage enough later to visit Novo Devitchi.

Nevertheless, the beauteous outburst of the unrivalled view repaid us. We should never take it again—by drosky—just as we should never go to Moscow again, unless invited to do so after an inexorable law put in force had sweetened its unsavoriness. But here we did see, once, Moscow as a panorama of superlative beauty. As we watched it from the side of the setting sun, it was like an Arabian Night's dream; like the heavenly Jerusalem let down from above, set with starry thrones, having gates of jasper and temples of gold. Everything of the disagreeable for the moment dropped out of mind, and here was the revered Mecca, one sight of which compels the Russian peasant, when approaching it, to drop quickly down upon his knees, and, with hat off, to cross himself with the most holy emotions!

A. V. D. HONEYMAN.

XII.

OUR LONGEST RAILWAY JOURNEY.

THE architectural ornaments of Moscow were too aërial for us; something on our own level would have been accepted with greater pleasure. If the streets had been gilded, instead of the churches, we might have felt more at ease. Nevertheless, many were the regrets expressed, when, on the evening of August 11, we took our departure from this portion of the Czar's dominion.

The hurry of seeing that the baggage was in the proper position, and the numerous endeavors to find our individual compartments in the railway coaches, prevented us from realizing that this was the last stopping place on strictly Russian territory, but as the train sped westward we turned to take a farewell glance at the city we had just left. Our gaze was rivected on one stupendous structure, whose massive domes rose from the gathering twilight, and cut their silhouettes against the golden light of declining day. This monument, standing as if to guard Moscow from all future intruders, was the "Temple of the Saviour," the "House of God," whose marble columns were carved in blood, and whose walls were reared to commemorate the sacrifice of human lives.

In three or four hours' time, between the long lines of berths and the odor of carbolic, the car reminded us of a "hospital on wheels," but our jovial porter (whose Russian blarney would shame an Irishman), succeeded in making our quarters as comfortable as possible, and we retired early, some to dream, maybe, of Pullman sleepers; others perhaps of our destination, which seemed so far in the distance. There was no dreaming and very little sleeping done that night, for at different stations along the route no less than nine Russians walked in and deposited themselves and baggage in that private car. Numerous demonstrations had no effect, neither would authoritative sentences hurled in plain English move them, and we were obliged to eject them by force. Whether they came to the conclusion that the Czar was traveling "incog.," or a party of anarchical strangers were speeding through the country, they finally gave the American part of the train a wide berth and retired to the rear.

The next morning, to our surprise and astonishment, every one was found literally buried beneath a layer of dust an inch in thickness, which had blown in through open doors and windows. If we had been on the Empire State express, running at seventy-five miles instead of one at the rate of thirty an hour, no one could have foretold what a tragedy might have occurred. The couches, which had looked so white and clean the previous evening, were now of a brownish hue, while the members of the party—well! they also had taken on the appearance of Russian pilgrims to Tartar shrines.

Astonishment is not a lasting numbness, and soon cries of "Dust my coat off," or "Send me a brush," were heard from all sides. Ten, twenty and even thirty kopeks were offered to those who would consent. Hereafter when we journey over the steppes of Russia it will be during a snowy winter, when the experience of being buried in furs, instead of dust, and warmly ensconced in a sleigh instead of a night train, will appeal more strongly to the American taste.

Reading and sleeping, alternately, with an occasional whisk broom accompaniment, passed the hours by, pleasantly for some. The more active members amused themselves by running to the doors at every town, and shouting in rapid and forcible German the usual question:

"Wie viel minuten bleiben, wie hier?" and whether they were answered or not, rushing pell-mell into the bouffet for soda-water and fruit cakes. "First come, first served," is the motto of those restaurants, and often the good and appetizing dainties would have disappeared before the less energetic ones had reached the scene of eating, and, at the third stroke of a bell, go off, with perhaps only a cheese sandwich.

These labored efforts soon ended, for at half-past ten P. M., nearly thirty hours after leaving Moscow, we entered the Polish city which was to be our home for a full day, and were driven rapidly from the station to the "Waldorf of Warsaw."

It was not long before the voice of the proprietor, calling out in loud and guttural accents, "Mrs. M. and the Misses M., Rooms 54 and 55," brought us to the overpowering realization that our railroad journey was ended. If we had remained another night aboard that sleeper those rusty sheets might have been again in evidence. There is no accounting for national peculiarities; all the gesticulating one might do would never make a Moscovite do otherwise than what he first intended. A bland smile is his only acquiescence; a shake of the head his only reply.

Our removal to the Hotel de l'Europe was a timely proceeding. The utter bewilderment of a hotel retinue when we chanced upon it was remarkable. It may have been the lateness of the hour, or the dazzling brilliancy of the red seals emblazoned on trunks, bags, and canvas rolls; in any event, this night, in particular, the employes seemed to lose their heads so entirely that an essayed pursuit of these unsuspecting natives was the only way that the owner of any hand luggage could get his share taken to his respective suite.

In regard to "Warszawa" itself, I cannot begin to extol its beauties. Those who have been there can judge for themselves of its attractiveness; those who have not could never appreciate what I might here relate. Suffice it to say, that this former capital, which was for generations the contesting ground of antagonistic countries, now compares favorably with any modernized city in the northern section of the continent. Though under the Czar's rule, the Poles abhor, and will not even mention, anything that is Russian. It seems rather sad to the representatives of a free land to see Poland subjugated by a foreign emperor, and the independence of its people forever crushed.

We left Warsaw with the anticipation that ere the morning of another day had dawned, we would have reached the German frontier. All hieroglyphical scrawls would have disappeared, and our passports, the bones not of contention, but of detention, would be scattered to the four winds, to fly as a sign to all those who there entered, that passports are a necessary means of admission. Still we lingered on the threshold of the Russian Empire to think that although it stands foremost among the nations of Europe, against the stoicism of whose defenders the forces of no united kingdoms can prevail, whose naval and maritime strongholds command the world, yet there was one event in its history which stirred the cities of the Czar and the inhabitants thereof into intense excitement. It was the arrival of a party of twenty-five American visitors.

EVELYN RANLETT MASON.

XIII.

BERLIN AND ITS ENVIRONS.

IN the early dawn of a dull gray morning, Saturday, August 14, 1897, the train from Warsaw reached the Friedrich Strasse station in the city of Berlin, and from it alighted the large majority of the Honeyman party. What had become of the others? In their anxiety to speedily terminate a long, tiresome ride, and a sleepless night, three had jumped off with bag and baggage at a suburban station, and the rest of us were now concerned as to when and how the manager would regain possession of them.

To retrace a little. When leaving Warsaw the previous afternoon it was believed that we would obtain a sleeping-car at Alexandrovo. But, alas, for human hopes! The sleeper was not to be obtained, and, worse than all, those of us who, by the paid favor of a train guard, had been assigned comfortable first-class compartments with the understanding that we should occupy them to Berlin if a sleeper were not secured, were ignominiously and with dispatch ushered out at this same Alexandrovo, to find second-class compartments as best we could. It was bad enough to fail in securing sleeping accommodations; it was adding insult to injury to be ejected from the quarters we had fairly secured to meet that emergency.

It was in this shuffle that our friends became separated from the rest of the party, and it was their anxiety to terminate so uncomfortable a journey, and their lack of familiarity with the German tongue and the city of Berlin, which occasioned their premature disembarkation.

But "all's well that ends well." We learned at the station that a train from the point at which they had alighted would soon follow us in; and so, with anxious expectancy, we summoned our Job-like qualities and stood guard about our ever-present luggage and awaited on the platform the coming of that train. A train did soon arrive, but our friends were not on it. A second one speedily followed, and then we found and welcomed them.

Once fairly started toward the hotel, American inquisitiveness began to forge to the front, and we began to look about us to see where we were and to learn what we could. Down the Friedrich Strasse we drove, and the large and substantial and fine buildings on either side drew our attention. One, who had seen Berlin before, remarked: "There is something about the appearance of this city which always reminds me of New York." To this a lady quickly responded: "Well, if Berlin is like New York, then I like it; but the dark atmosphere now rather reminds me of Chicago." That carriage load unanimously concluded, however, that, whether like New York or Chicago, or both, Berlin was entitled to and should receive hearty approval. And, as if to toast us for that sentiment, our attention was just then drawn to a large corner saloon, with a window conspicuously advertising "American Drinks."

Emerging into Unter den Linden, with its broader vista and brighter air, our spirits rose still higher, and we reached the Hotel du Nord in good humor, prepared to accept any reasonable disposition of us that might be made. But even an angelic mood is hardly proof against being assigned to the rear end of the top floor in a house where no "ascenseur" is to be found; and so there were some demands and firm protestations until desired changes were made. The accommodating spirit of the affable portier was then gratefully acknowledged and all was again serene.

Just here, why is it that landlords so generally assign the incoming guests to the most undesirable rooms? Are they so constituted that they must first gauge American travelers by such an ordeal? Or is it a part of their business to endeavor first to dispose of the rooms one would not seek? It would seem that a contrary course would be the wiser, would please the guests better, would save the landlord annoyance and trouble, and would preserve the amiability of both. It would then be as it should be, first come, best served; and late comers could have no good ground for complaint.

A hasty toilet followed by a good breakfast put all in fair condition, mentally and physically, for the day. A necessary preliminary to active work yet demanded attention—a visit to the Dresdner Bank, or to the office of a representative of Messrs. Henry Gaze & Sons, for cash. At the latter place we were charged a commission for cashing travelers checks—an unwarranted commission. And it was done in such a deceptive way as to convince us that it was a deliberately planned imposition.

When one comes to record the doings of but a single day, how many little incidents are noted, trivial in themselves, perhaps, but involving important principles and influencing the habits and lives of people.

Now, however, we were at last ready for action, and it was thought advisable, particularly since the threatening early hours had now brought the dampening rain, to visit the palaces so conveniently near. A few of us took a guide, the only one the hotel could give us at the moment, whose employment no one would subsequently admit, and we paraded first (and last as it proved) to the residence of the late Emperor William. This building, so full of warm interest by reason of the personality of that admirable man, is now little more than a storehouse for the bric-a-brac, and photographs, and furniture, and presents of that household. A peculiar interest attaches to that window made historical by the Emperor's habit of there appearing to the view of his admiring subjects; and the again and again repeated echoes, to more than a score of times, of the concert or music hall were wonderful and interesting. Apart from these two items little of interest was found. It may be that the slowness, age, weak voice and listless manner of our guide were largely responsible for this. At all events when we emerged from that palace, all by common consent, and without a word, demurely retraced steps to the hotel, and palace-seeing was abandoned.

The Berlin stores proved unusually attractive, and great were the planning and hunting and bargaining for those numerous little things which would as gifts to friends at home prove that they were not forgotten by us, although so far away. And in this pleasant occupation our friend from "way down in Maine" here discovered the greatest novelty of all, one in which the ladies took an interest and even invested some funds, to wit, a patent cork-screw, which is not a screw at all, although it effectually does the work of one, but which looks like, what one of our home friends insisted it must be, a whistle, or mouth-organ, or some kind of a musical instrument. Its mysteries explained and a trial of its utility made, it was discovered that the only music it can produce is that of the suddenly released cork.

"Unter den Linden" was a disappointment.

Not that it is not a fine city street, but that it is no finer than many others, and not nearly so attractive and pretty as some. Wilhelm Strasse, where several of the princes and foreign ambassadors reside, and Friedrich Strasse and Leipziger Strasse are prettier streets. The lindens are not choice specimens, the roadways are not the best paved—one side is but cobbled; the walks under the trees are neither smooth nor clean, and the buildings generally are of no special merit. There are points of beauty and interest along the street, but taken as a whole it is disappointing.

The palaces present no specially attractive features. This is particularly the case with the one used by the present Emperor. It looks as though a good New England house-cleaning, inside and out, were greatly needed. This is due in part to its age, partly to the dark stone employed in its construction, and partly to the dirt and smoke of that great city. In front of this palace are a very fine monument and semi-circular peristyle, not yet entirely completed, erected by the nation in memory of Emperor William the Great. At the side of the palace is the Palace Spring Fountain, a large, unique, and attractive work. The Monument of Victory and the Brandenburg gate are also beautiful works of art, and the new Parliament building is large and handsome. Many fine monuments are scattered throughout the city, and parks and gardens and squares are numerous and attractive.

The Thiergarten is particularly so. It is a very large forest, as dense as in some mountain wild, almost in the heart of the city, with broad avenues cut out and lakes scattered here and there. By stepping only a few feet off from a busy street one can there find the shade and seclusion of a virgin forest.

Schools, academies and colleges abound, and galleries and museums for every art and treasure are on every hand. The education of the people in all useful, elevating, historical, and technical branches is amply provided for and encouraged. It is, therefore, no wonder that German mentality and cultivation are so high.

But what should be said about the beer gardens, so numerous and so extensive? They form part of the life and business, and of the education also, of the city, and are rendered as attractive and bright as lights and music and flowers can make them. And not gardens only, but halls also, large and airy, and brilliant in colors and illumination. And yet, with them all, one sees less intemperance than can be witnessed nearly every day in almost any one of our numerous American barrooms. Why is this?

Poverty is not in evidence in Berlin. If it does exist—and it is hardly possible that it does not—it is well hidden. Not a single mendicant was seen. A comprehensive drive in both the old and new parts of the city, and extending into the suburbs, and walks around by day and night, disclosed no poor quarter. The people dress nicely, look clean and tidy, appear industrious, and deport themselves in a most respectable manner. The city is altogether beautiful, and apparently prosperous and progressive.

A drive to Charlottenburg is inviting, and a visit to the mausoleum in the garden of the Royal Palace should not be omitted. The sculptured figures upon the sarcophagi of the illustrious dead are wonderful masterpieces, and the marble drapery is simply a marvel of the sculptor's art. While waiting for the appearance of the official who issues the tickets of admission to the mausoleum, we were considerably entertained by the maneuvers of the soldiers on duty at that point. The guards were about being changed, and the relief was marshaled in front of the barracks. When the order to march was given the men started off with such a quick, high, jerky step that it was for all the world as if they had been prodded unexpectedly in the rear with a sharp bayonet, or were endeavoring to kick a receding foe in front of them. The spectator was unable at the moment to tell whether the movement would develop into a run or subside into a recognized march. The latter proved to be the case, but the reason for such a movement at all is obscure.

A visit to Berlin must always include a trip to Potsdam. That busy town with its royal castle, extensive barracks, historical lime tree, the Friedens-Kirche, and the park and palace of Sans Souci and the new palace is both attractive and instructive. No one can look upon the old lime tree, so carefully preserved and protected, without an accompanying mental vision of the suppliants who there from time to time made known to Frederick the Great their various wants and grievances, and implored his aid and intervention. And then going to the old wind mill, another picture of a totally different type is presented, and we view the sturdy old owner persisting in and insisting upon his individual rights against the desire and the temptation of the proffered gold of the same famous potentate, and thereby retaining the ownership and possession of his chosen property. Can it be doubted that the sovereign, notwithstanding his disappointment, really entertained in consequence more consideration and greater respect for that subject? It was but a notable exhibition of that manly independence which must be the basis of all good and stable government.

The great fountain in the park is fine, but the view from it up the six great terraces to the palace of Sans Souci is a prettier sight. The flowers and fruit and shrubbery on these terraces are so abundant as to completely hide the soil upon and against which they stand, and are so carefully tended and trained, and so bright and various in colors as to form a beautiful foundation of great height upon which the palace appears to rest. And a view from the palace over the park discloses a pretty landscape. The palace itself is not beautiful, and in character reminds one rather of the long, low, rambling buildings of the negro quarters of a southern plantation "befo' de wah." It is quite near to this palace that the old wind mill stands, and then the Orangery,

Paradise Garden, Japanese House, Italian Villa and the Mausoleum follow. At the rear of the palace, up the steep ascent, leading directly to the center of the building, is the road by which Napoleon entered, and he occupied rooms in the Royal Castle in the town.

Not far from Sans Souci is the New Palace, now occupied by the royal family. It is very large, decidedly Dutch in its architecture and wholly unattractive in appearance. The interior is in no respect equal to the Russian palaces at St. Petersburg and Moscow. The only apartment worthy of special note is the shell room, which is large and unique in style, and built entirely of shells and small pieces of valuable stones arranged in odd and quaint designs. It is here, we are told, that the family hold their Christmas and other similar festivities.

It was a surprise to us all to see in Berlin the exceedingly large grounds of the Grecian Embassy, and we could but wonder how so small a country came to have so extensive a foothold there, and what effect, if any, such exhibition of that foreign power had on the action of Germany with reference to the Cretan troubles.

In Moscow we had marveled when we found

the edges of the under sheets on our beds well filled with buttonholes, and the edges of the quilts above us well supplied with buttons; but one of our ladies solved the enigma by declaring the purpose to be to button the occupant in at night. At Warsaw we found the upper sheet nicely buttoned some six or eight inches over the edges of the quilts. And in Berlin we failed at first to find any quilt at all on the beds, but finally discovered it completely covered and buttoned in the upper sheet, as is a pillow in its case. We thought if this progressive habit should follow us to Amsterdam that we would there find bed and all encased securely in some novel garment. But we left the custom at Berlin, fortunately, where the difficulty of extracting a heavy quilt from its case, in order to leave only sufficient covering for a summer night, was so great after the fatigue of a day's sight-seeing or shopping that we had no longing for further similar experiences.

Of the exactions of the Custom House officials and their aversion to paper and predilection for cotton and linen goods others can speak (if not permitted to write) with more knowledge and feeling. Likewise regarding the attractions of the Apollo Theatre and the

Panopticum. The Raths-Keller, noted as one of the sights of Berlin, is not to be compared, except in extent, with that in the Betz building in Philadelphia. And here it was that the Teuton of our party sought to use his knowledge of the German tongue for the benefit of himself and friends, called a waiter, and, with great deliberation and distinctness, so that even we almost understood his words, gave an order for some refreshments. The waiter smiled and, with great politeness and in the best English, replied, "If you would like to learn to speak German, come to my house tomorrow morning and I will give you a lesson." It proved that he had no ear for "Pennsylvania Dutch;" and we discovered that he had spent several years in America. And this was not the only incident of such a character during our trip.

The cab drivers are numerous, capable, and accommodating. They are so anxious to please, that one, I am told, with a lady and a gentleman for a fare, who positively declined all the attractions of theater and museum and garden he tendered them, finally concluded that they must be seeking only the society and peculiar attractions of each other, and he thereupon drove them slowly and carefully in side streets and shaded lanes, and the dark roads of the parks, without a word from them, or a glance back at them, until they at last woke to the fact that cabby was "on to their little game." Then, by using a mixture of English and French, and Pennsylvania Dutch, in all which no word of gratitude was found, they eventually succeeded in being driven to their hotel. Ungrateful wretches. Wonder who they were!

We were delighted to reach Berlin and enjoyed every moment of our sojourn there. We left it early Tuesday morning, August 17, with considerable regret. It is altogether an interesting city. We found the Hotel du Nord to be conveniently located and well managed, with an excellent table and accommodating officials. Our hope is that we may be able to visit Berlin again under equally pleasant circumstances and for a longer stay.

NATHANIEL EWING.

XIV.

A DAY IN AMSTERDAM.

AFTER a pleasant trip of almost 400 miles from Berlin through the ever-changing stretches of delightful country, we arrived, August 17, at the Central Railway station on the "Y" in Amsterdam, on the north side of the city, at 8:27 P. M., and were soon comfortably quartered in the large and commodious "Victoria Hotel," near by, at the corner of the Damrak and Prins Hendrikkade. Here we did full justice to an elegant dinner that had been prepared and was waiting for us, and for which our long trip had most successfully prepared our party, except a few of us with delicate appetites. The next day it rained—the first rainy day of our experience abroad.

Amsterdam, the commercial capital of Holland, is said to be as good as Venice, with a super-added humor which gives the sightseer the most singular zest and pleasure. You can scarcely fancy a run through Pekin to be more odd, strange and yet familiar. There were perceptible a rush and prodigious vitality; an immense swarm of life, busy waters crowded with barges, spacious markets teeming with people, the ever-wonderful Jew's quarter, a "dear old world of painting and of the past," yet alive and throbbing and palpable, actual and yet passing before you swiftly and strangely as a dream.

This wonderful city lies at the influx of the Amstel into the "Y" or "IJ," which is an arm of the Zuiderzee, which has been formed into an excellent harbor. The town was founded at the beginning of the Thirteenth Century, when Gysbrecht II. built a castle here in 1204 and constructed the dam, which gave the town its name. In 1275 Count Florens V. granted the town exemption from the imposts of Holland and Zeeland, and in 1311 it was finally united with Holland. In the Fourteenth Century the town began to assume greater importance, and at the beginning of the Spanish troubles it had become a very important city. In 1490 the Emperor Maximilian I. gave the city the privilege of using the imperial crown as the crest in its armorial bearings.

The real importance and prosperity of Amsterdam date from the close of the Sixteenth Century, when the Spanish war had ruined Antwerp, and the horrors of the inquisition had compelled numbers of enterprising merchants and skillful manufacturers to seek a new home in Holland. Between 1585 and 1595 the town was nearly doubled in extent and was greatly favored by Prince Maurice of Orange. The conclusion of peace shortly afterward and the establishment of the East India Company combined to raise Amsterdam within a very short period to the rank of the greatest mercantile city on the continent. After the dissolution of the Dutch Republic, Amsterdam became the residence of King Louis Napoleon, in 1808. The population now is about 500,000. The commercial trade of Amsterdam is very important, though the number of ships that enter and clear the harbor is scarcely a third of that at Antwerp.

Its industries are also considerable, including sugar and camphor refineries, tobacco and cobalt-blue manufactories, and diamond polishing mills. The principal attractions of Amsterdam are Rijks Museum, Fodor Museum, Zoological Gardens, walks on the De Ruyterkade, Oosterdok, and Westerdok; the Delft depot and Kalverstraat, the principal shopping street, which leads southward from "The Dam" and is one of the chief thoroughfares of the city, notwithstanding its entire width is little, if any more than just the sidewalks of some of the streets in New York and other of our American cities. After nine P. M. this street becomes the scene of a kind of Corso or promenade, occupied and used almost exclusively by pedestrians.

By reason of canals running through the business streets of the city, it is divided into ninety islands, which are connected by nearly 300 bridges. The depth of the water in these canals is about five feet, below which is said to be a layer of mud of about equal thickness. To prevent malarial exhalations the water is renewed by an arm of the North Sea Canal, while the mud is removed by dredges. Some of the canals are lined with avenues of elms and present a pleasant, and in places a handsome and picturesque appearance. The houses are all constructed on foundations of piles, a fact which gave rise to the jest of Erasmus of Rotterdam, that he knew a city whose inhabitants dwelt in the tops of trees like rooks. The upper stratum of the natural soil is loose sand upon which no permanent building can be erected, unless a solid substructure be first formed by driving piles about twenty feet long into the firmer sand beneath. The operations of the builder below the surface of the ground are frequently as expensive as those above it.

The focus of the business life of the city is a large square called "The Dam." It owes its name to its position on the west side of the old embankment with which the foundation and name of the city are traditionally connected. It is surrounded by the Exchange, the Royal Palace, the New Church, and several private homes, and is the center from which the principal tramways and streets diverge. Of the buildings surrounding the square the Royal Palace (Het Paleis) is the most imposing and important. It was begun in 1648 as a town hall and substantially finished in 1655 at a cost of 8,000,000 florins.

It rests on a foundation of 13,659 piles, about twenty feet long. It was presented by the city to King Louis Napoleon as a residence in 1808. It was by reason of its location well adapted for a town hall, but, having no principal entrance and being situated in the open market place, it is unsuitable for a palace. All the apartments are richly adorned with sculptures in white marble, which produce an imposing effect. It is one of the grand homes of Wilhelmina, the popular Queen of Holland.

We were fortunate on all sides in our opportunities of seeing nobility and royalty; however, but a few of our party were so happily favored as to have a view of Queen Wilhelmina, than whom no royal princess of the present age has been discussed with more interest, nor has been more of a puzzle to the diplomats of Europe. She is young, talented, accomplished, beautiful, of unequaled lineage, and the sovereign of 35,000,000 of people. All the crowned heads of Europe consider her a prize well worth striving for; and no wonder that every princeling desires to become a consort to such a queen. And with such accomplishments we are not certain, but that, with sufficient encouragement, other than princelings might be induced to turn their heads and hearts in that direction.

This young princess is not yet Queen. She will assume that dignity upon attaining her eighteenth year, which will be August 31, 1898. The name of Queen Wilhelmina is everywhere spoken with enthusiasm. Three centuries of tradition; three hundred years of all that is grand and glorious in the history of this proud Empire center in their Virgin Queen. Her picture is seen everywhere, and it is said that half of the girl babies in the country are called Wilhelmina.

It is not commonly known that Holland claims to be the second colonial power in the world. This is the secret of her present prosperity. The average wealth of each citizen is three times as much as that of England. To the Queen of this Empire is given an annual salary of two hundred thousand dollars, every cent of which is spent by the young princess in the cause of charity. Of course, she can well afford to do without this salary, as she is said to be one of the richest sovereigns in the world, being sole heir to the entire wealth of the Empire and the estate of all the Nassaus.

Rijks Museum is an important building covering nearly three acres of ground, erected in 1877-'85, in the early Dutch Renaissance style. The exterior is adorned and ornamented with mosaic decorations representing the figures and events in the history of Dutch art. To the artist the interior arrangement is perfect and is a veritable paradise. We cannot go into details to any extent more than to say that the collections include not only the paintings, drawings and engravings formerly in the Royal Museum at the Trippenhuis, and in the Museum van der Hoop, but also various pictures and other works of art collected from the Stadhuis, the Huiszittenhuis and elsewhere, and the art industrial collections of the old Dutch Museum at the Hague and of the Antiquarium Society at Amsterdam. The Museum is surrounded with pleasure grounds and enclosed by a tastefully wrought iron railing.

The Zoological Garden is one of the finest in Europe and little inferior to that of London. It covers 28 acres and is well worth the two to three hours' time it requires to make a visit through it. The diamond polishing establishments, the many quaint and neatly kept shops lining the narrow streets and ways along the canals, exhibiting fine collections of freshly polished diamonds and many other precious stones and wares, disturbing the peace and quiet of our already overburdened trunks and bags and depleted purses, were attractive and interesting to the extent of maintaining our usual enthusiasm to see the sights, regardless of the gloom and moisture attending that morning's Dutch downpour. None of our party visited all of the interesting places of this quaint old city, yet some one or more spent considerable time in the above named and other places with pleasure and profit, not, however, of a financial character.

The principal environ of Amsterdam is Zaandam, a town of about 20,000 inhabitants, situated about six miles from Amsterdam at the influx of the Zaan in the "Y." It is a thriving little city, thoroughly Dutch in appearance. Our trip down to this place in the afternoon was a very pleasant and delightful one. It certainly was through the land of the wind-mills, as it is said there are about 400 on the banks of the Zaan, between these two cities; being used for many different purposes, comprising oil, saw, corn, paint, cement and papermills, as well as, also, to pump water from the lowlands over dykes back into the Zaan. The surface of the Zaan is several feet above the level of the surrounding country, which is protected from overflow only by means of these embankments.

The Zaandam Dutch were holding high carnival this day. It was the two-hundredth anniversary of the arrival of Peter the Great of Russia. He came hither in the dress of a common workman, under the name Peter Michaelof, and worked as a ship carpenter, with a view of acquiring a practical knowledge of the art, in order to impart it to his countrymen.

The hut of Peter the Great, situated on Krimpstraat, is the principal attraction at Zaandam. It is a rude wooden structure, now protected and preserved by a substantial brick building surrounding it and belonging to the Czar of Russia. On the front of this brick building, over the entrance, is a tablet bearing the inscription: "Het Czaarpeter huisje is hedur voor het publick gesloten. Het Consulaat-Generaal van Rusland," which, in consequence of the many recent gymnastic linguistic performances of the H. P. T's was easily understood and translated. The interior of this hut consists of two small rooms and a bed closet. A marble slab over the chimney place, bearing the inscription "Petro Magno Alexander," was placed there by Emperor Alexander, on the occasion of his visit, in 1814. Another is the one connected with the visit of the Czarewitch, in 1839. In consequence of the nautical phraseology of Russia being mainly of Dutch origin, these people look upon their city and this little hut as the fountain head of the great and powerful Russian navy of to-day.

A Day in Amsterdam.

It was surely a gala occasion, comparing with the American circus or country fair day. The fathers and mothers, beaux and belles and the thousands of school children of this city, as well as others from Amsterdam, thronged and flooded the principal streets of the place. They were dressed in the most weird, unique and fantastic costumes, to be described only by an expert. The prevailing headdress among the women was a sort of helmet, of brass, fitting close over the head, decorated with lace and ribbons draped and looped in all sorts of weird, decorative styles. The balance of their outfit, ending in the regulation wooden shoe, cut from a block of elm or linden, was equally and strangely novel.

And the costumes worn by some of the men will be called to the minds of the party by comparing them with the worst fitting suit of bloomers they ever saw on an amateur bicycle rider.

This little side excursion will long be remembered by the members of our party as one of the most interesting and instructive of the many little trips of this kind suggested and provided by our genial and wide-awake Manager. Amusing incidents of one kind or another happened almost every day and August

18 was no exception. It loomed up with one that, doubtless, would be classed under the list of "Another"; and will be called to mind to those who were unfortunate enough to witness it, by the exclamation of the gentleman who was acting in the capacity of guide or escort to the crowd on our return from Zaandam, from the steamer to the hotel, when, after attracting and directing the attention of the party, he said "O, my Heavens! Isn't that awful!! What will they think of me!!!"

As the day and evening drew to a close and the time for our departure came near, feeling that we had spent a very pleasant and profitable time in this quaint old city, there still remained for those of us who were fortunate enough to be in the parlors of our hotel the most interesting and entertaining feature of our stay in Amsterdam, when the accomplished and talented Miss Evelyn R. Mason recited for us, among other selections, the charming and very appropriate poem of Eugene Field, entitled, "In Amsterdam," in a manner so pleasing and effective as to leave no question in our minds as to her ability as an artist, nor of the fact that Eugene Field certainly had been in Amsterdam and on the Kalverstraat in the capacity of a tourist.

So ended our stay in this city and we left it the night of August 18 with a consciousness of regret bordering on delight, feeling that "it had been good for us to be here," and that our Manager had made no mistake in including it in our itinerary. The day will always stand out as a bright one in our many memory gems of the H. P. T. of 1897, for we can assure our friends that in touring Europe their recollections will necessarily have to be tinged with a shadow of regret, unless they shall spend at least "A Day in Amsterdam."

R. E. UMBEL AND W. J. JOHNSON.

XV.

AT THE HAGUE.

THE Holland capital has always seemed to me to be one of the most restful and delightful of the smaller cities of Europe. The people there are not quite so Dutchy as at Amsterdam or Rotterdam—one should not dislike it if they were, because when you are in Holland you expect the inhabitants to do what only the Dutch will do, and they are a most interesting people with it all—and there is an air of refinement about the place and its surroundings. There is no jarring upon your sense of the fitness of things, as you walk through its broad squares or shop in its tidy stores. A prettiness and tidiness and a real solid comfort are to be found everywhere. If I were not a resident of America, I should like to live at The Hague.

And you have plenty of history and plenty of poetry in this home of William of Orange; while out on the sea-beach near by is the cleanest, neatest, and, in many respects, most attractive bathing place on the Continent.

We stopped at the Hotel Paulez, just opposite in a diagonal line from the older Vieux Doelen. The Vieux Doelen is a more fashionable hotel, where many of the aristocratic people of Europe board for a month or two at a time in the summer season. We observed that our new American Ambassador was wise enough to go there, for we happened to notice on the afternoon succeeding our arrival that the Royal carriage of the Queen came for him, in real court style, with postilions in livery, to take him to an audience with Her Majesty. The Paulez, however, was quiet, and had few other guests, and we enjoyed its comfortable rooms, though not the tardiness of its meals. The electric tramcar passes the door, and furnishes an example of the perfection of street travel by electric power. What is said to be impracticable in America is here demonstrated to be entirely feasible, for there are no trolley wires, but simply a noiseless carriage running over steel rails at a pace fast or slow, at the will of the motorman. Each car has a first and a second-class compartment, at very cheap fares, and either one is more cosy and comfortable than our American electric cars.

There are just four attractions at The Hague which I always want to see when visiting this city. The one, least important, of course, but not least interesting, is the old Pickle Woman's Stand, in the market place. She is the same smart, good-natured lady who was there in 1874, when I first made her acquaintance, though possibly it is her daughter who now serves the patrons. She has no business by day to speak of, and, therefore, I would not then walk around the corner to see her, if, indeed, she is there at all when the sun is shining. But when nine o'clock in the evening arrives, and the young Dutch mynheers and dames are on promenade, then her booth becomes the center of a scene of earnest work which is delightful to observe. She has a goodly lot of jars of small pickles and several heaped-up baskets of hard-boiled eggs. These are all she sells, but an array of white shells upon the ground, like fallen blossoms of cherry orchards in May, gleam under the electric lights, as the scores of her customers stand around eating, first a pickle, then an egg, and so alternating until six, seven, or a dozen of each are duly swallowed. It goes to prove that the true Dutchman's stomach is as enduring as leather, and I learn that, because of his irreproachable conscience, these small things in no wise disturb his night's rest. This one woman, with her eggs and pickles, would kill off all the younger population of an American settlement, but at The Hague, where everybody has been brought up on them, they are simply appetizers, and the young men rise up next morning fresh and hearty to push the trekschuits, and the young dames still earlier to scrub anew the front doorsills.

The second and more pathetic sight is the Binnenhof; the seat of the Dutch Parliament, with its ancient hall of the States of the time of the Republic. Here, in front of it, on that bright May morning in 1649, brave John of Barneveld, the great advocate of Holland, "whose errors were so few and whose virtues were so great," laid down his head upon the block, though past seventy years of age, simply because he did not belong to the men of that generation. Here in this square and around it were born so much of Holland liberty and so much of princely valor that we Americans, who have patterned our patriotism after these splendid old Netherlanders, should never leave this interesting city without reverently standing before this sacred spot.

A third attractive place is the Picture Gallery, or the Royal Museum, in the Maurits Huis, where are a half dozen or more really great Dutch paintings; one of them known the world over as Paul Potter's Bull (though I don't care one snap for that bull, while I do admire the gentle, patient, perfectly-presented cow by his side), and another the chef dœuvre of Paul Rembrandt, usually spoken of as "The Lesson in Anatomy." There is here some of the best work of Jan Steen, and I do not know where else he can be studied to better advantage.

The fourth interesting spot to me is the Royal Palace. Not that it contains anything worth looking at to one who has seen real palaces at St. Petersburg, or Versailles, or Potsdam, or even Dröttningholm; but rather because it is so simple and unroyal. It even adjoins the shops of the street on which it stands, without so much as an alley between. It is the plainest abode of royalty in civilized lands. But it is homelike within and has an air of business-like comfort without.

We did not enter the Palace; and, in fact,

The Young Holland Queen.

Wilhelmina, born August 31, 1880, will ascend the throne in her own right August 31, 1898. Her mother, Princess Emma, has been Queen Regent since the death of William III. in 1890. She is much beloved by her people, who are looking forward with great interest to her taking the crown.

could not, for the full-flown flag overhead showed that the Queen was in residence. But I have heretofore wandered over its hard floors and enjoyed its inelegant comeliness, and this time I had the good fortune, while inquiring concerning the movements of its occupants, to see the youthful and pretty Queen Wilhelmina herself come up to its large front doors in a plain, though red-lined, landau, with two attractive horses, and saw the sweet and dignified bow with which she always greets her subjects when they unlift hats in her presence. She was full of grace and as beautiful as fair. The Queen Dowager was at her side, a woman of no marked features, dressed in black. Others of the party also saw, later, at the railway station, this first-named little lady, who, next year, in August, when eighteen years of age, will take the crown, and, it is to be hoped, win to herself more than ever the love of all her people. We voted her a handsome, happy, sensible, womanly girl, and may her reign be long and her pathway strewed with flowers! She has some of the best blood of the Kingdom in her veins, and while hers is a nation small in numbers, how rich it is in the world's best virtues!

As you walk about this city, so new and yet

a full century older than New York, the bright, new arcade of shops, the smooth pavements, the quiet fish-pond, the picturesque Town Hall, the well-shaded streets continue to speak of peace, prosperity and plenty, and one need not wonder that the rich merchants of the little kingdom like to come to The Hague and end their days on the Lange Voorhout, when they are tired of poring over their East India ledgers.

The surroundings of The Hague are quite as attractive as the city's interior; perhaps more so. One has but to drive to the Palace in the Wood, so long inhabited by the former Queen, who could not live in peace with her husband, with its shady avenues, intersected by canals; or drive to Scheveningen, to see that art and nature have combined to give beauty to this "largest village of Europe," where, as said an old Dutch author, there is "a tree, a flower and a bird for each of its 160,000 inhabitants." At the Palace in the Wood there are walls adorned with satin needlework; hangings and floors with costly needlework carpets; paintings by Van Dyck and Jordaens and the school of Rubens; splendid Japanese furnishings and plenty of romantic stories connected with each of its two-and-a-half century possessors. The umbrageous trees cover fish ponds and larger lakes and pleasant walks. The carriages of the wealthy and the feet of the poor go to and fro without supervision of police or, worse, of newspaper reporters. For it must be understood that The Hague, and, in fact, nearly all Holland, is so law-abiding, the inhabitants are so peaceable, that the jails are empty!

At Scheveningen our ladies enjoyed thoroughly an hour or two in the sun chairs upon the beach, watching the bathing wagons and bathers, and the rippling waves and far-away sails. There was a strong wind blowing from the east, but the sun shone brightly, and within these covered chairs came quiet and rest and a sense of genuine pleasure. There is not in Europe a cleaner, wholesomer, more restful place than on this brick-paved beach, in sight of the spot where occurred one of the finest Dutch naval victories that history records. When De Ruyter whipped both the English and French navies, Holland was at its zenith of glory.

Did you ever read garrulous Sam. Pepy's "Diary"? If you did, you remember how he danced attendance upon Charles the Second, when that historic character, of handsome figure but graceless morals, embarked at Scheveningen to take possession of the English throne. And here it was that Englishmen flocked to beg Prince William of Orange to accept the crown of their misgoverned island. I doubt not that, when Chesterfield was Ambassador to Holland, and when Louis Bonaparte held sway under the great Napoleon's tenure, this beach, as sandy and solid as now, the waves before it just as yellow-green and the air above it just as brisk and penetrating, captivated and charmed as it does to-day. It is a spot for rest, for meditation and for holy resolves.

Once upon a time the writer left The Hague on the canal aboard a trekschuit and went to Delft. It was in a day when Delft ware was not so much sought after in America as now, and was comparatively little known. The journey was taken simply to have the restful feeling of being towed along the canal by man-power (for some of the distance by a horse) and to observe how the Dutch passed their time in garden, back-yard and field, for we skimmed slowly along by each in turn. Then, as now, the country meadows were dotted with myriads of the choicest cattle. The sights were numerous, novel, humorous, instructive. It was an experience never to be forgotten.

And so my one regret now is that the shortness of the time prevented the party of 1897 from going upon just such a journey over to Delft, or to Leyden. It is one of the easiest things to do in Holland, the most natural and most interesting, but something few travelers endeavor to accomplish. When next we come to this land of Queen Wilhelmina, let us, first, in the evening, all visit the old woman in the market square, and, next day, take the trekschuit for a six-mile pull, as our Holland forefathers formerly did for at least ten generations.

A. V. D. HONEYMAN.

XVI.

HOMEWARD BOUND.

DARK and dreary dawned the morning of August 21, the day we were to turn our faces toward our native land and leave behind the places where two very delightful months had been spent.

As we left the wharf at Antwerp and began the passage down the treacherous river Scheldt, we saw anchored the American man-of-war "San Francisco," whose band on deck was playing "Auld Lang Syne," but, as their gaze traveled over to the "Friesland" and they saw the numerous American flags being frantically waved over the railing, the tune changed to one of Sousa's most charming two-steps, the "Washington Post."

Every one rose with alacrity when the bugle call sounded for luncheon, and I am sure not a few upon leaving the saloon wondered whether dinner would seem equally inviting.

That morning we remained on deck to watch the funny little Dutch towns, as they came in view, with the unique aspect of the dykes enclosing them. Some hours later we saw our river pilot depart in his row boat, and then we passed into the North Sea and through the Dover Straits.

Dinner was well attended, with the exception of those who concluded the air was more refreshing on deck.

Sunday morning we were passing the chalk cliffs of England, well on our way toward the ocean. We were much disappointed when on entering the saloon to find there was to be no service. We had one or two ministers on board, but possibly the effects of mal-de-mer prevented their making any attempt to get farther than the deck. At all events, so we thought, but when the next Sunday the same neglect was repeated, we thought—otherwise.

In the afternoon the Lizard was passed and shortly after we saw the Lily light, our last glimpse of land.

Monday the good ship was making labored efforts to ride the gigantic waves, which rose about her and, in consequence, forcing many of her passengers to remain below. Meals were poorly attended and even books held no attraction.

In the afternoon a terrific gale came on, and by night the rain was falling in torrents. A few of the more courageous ones remained on deck with rugs wrapped tightly about them and umbrellas as shields from the rain and waves.

Just here let me say the ginger snaps and soda crackers now gave out, and those whose appetites had withstood the pitching and rolling were forced to content themselves with lemons and an occasional orange.

Tuesday, Wednesday, Thursday and Friday passed by with rapidity. There were good times; some high seas, but not to kick up much of a frolic with the passengers. Occasional games of "shuffle board" and "ring toss" were tried and a few regularly gathered in the saloon when evening came on to play "whist" and wait till lemonade and sandwiches were passed around at nine o'clock.

Few and far between were the sunsets, as fog reigned supreme, and, I think, when the time came for clearing the decks, there was nothing to clear but chairs.

Saturday was spent in the usual quiet way

until evening, when preparations began for a dance on the port deck. Benches and chairs were removed and the sides were first enclosed with large sheets of canvas and then covered with the different national flags. Electric lights were arranged artistically and the piano held an important place. All this was due to the captain's thoughtfulness and generosity. At eight the dancing began, and everything was entirely satisfactory—except the music. A man was finally discovered who played the violin, but after one or two efforts he retired highly disgusted with his own performance. After that a few desultory attempts were made and then two men made their appearance from the steerage with accordions. Dancing progressed finely until half-past ten, when it was interrupted by the serving of refreshments. A little more dancing—and people retired from the scene of action to claim a much needed rest after their undue exertions.

Sunday numerous remarks were flying about that we would not get in until Tuesday morning, as the run for the past three days had been "very poor," and anxiously did everyone await the coming of the chart. By noon the crowd was almost impenetrable, and as the first one caught a glimpse of "390 miles," our longest run, a wild halloo of joy went up, and we knew the morrow would see us safely landed.

Many of the ocean-lovers who had made bets concerning the run were highly disappointed, but they were in the minority.

Sunday afternoon the bell tolled for a fire drill and the jolly tars put to with a will. One poor fellow, miscalculating his distance (and when once in place he could not stir), received for ten minutes the full volume of water from the largest hose.

Monday, at eleven o'clock, we saw the most welcome sight to Americans homeward bound, Fire Island, with its spiral lighthouse and long stretch of sandy beach just visible through the mist; it looked, indeed, its welcome.

Then confusion reigned throughout the ship, trunks were hauled up out of the hold, lusty shouts were heard from the sailors fore and aft, steamer trunks were busily packed, umbrellas, rugs and cushions strapped, while constant calling after the different stewards made a good accompaniment.

Soon Sandy Hook came in sight and the "Friesland" stopped to take on the pilot, who was to steer us through the intricacies of the bay. As he came on board a grand rush was made to secure the New York papers he brought with him.

Luncheon was served at 1.30, instead of 12, and I am going to add a word in favor of our table steward. All future passengers, who have the good fortune of sitting at the captain's table on the "Friesland" and who are waited upon by the assistant steward, will scarcely find a more polite, obliging and well educated man. So, in fact, are all the stewards, but he was an exception in some particulars.

After luncheon we bade adieu to those whom we had been associated with so long. It seemed rather sad, now that we had reached home, to say "good-bye" to those friends who had shared our comforts and discomforts on the other side of the Atlantic. Leaning over the rail of the vessel, as she slowly wended her way up the bay, were those who were coming to America for the first time; others who had been visiting their own country and were returning; and still others, like ourselves, who gazed toward the coast of Long Island and realized that,

> "Though on foreign shores we may roam,
> Be it ever so far away,
> There's no place like 'Home.'"

The remembrances of the eternal cities of the Czar, the Empire of Kaiser Wilhelm, even the realms of Queen Victoria, all faded from our minds when we beheld the high and lofty buildings of New York city. The sovereign colors of the mighty nations of Europe blended in one more glorious emblem, the Stars and Stripes.

At three P. M., as the "Friesland" lowered her gangplank and we stepped upon an American pier, did we not think of the oft repeated verse:

"Breathes there a man with soul so dead,
That never to himself hath said
This is my own, my native land?"

ADÈLE S. MASON.

MEMBERS OF PARTY.

Barry, Mrs. Frances H., Wilmington, Del.
Bennett, Rev. William R., Madison, N. J.
Chase, Mr. Louis A., Plainfield, N. J.
Coit, Mrs. Alfred, New London, Conn.
Donnell, Capt. E. P., Bath, Me.
Donnell, Mrs. E. P., Bath, Me.
Donnell, Mrs. Jennie C., Bath, Me.
Estil, Mr. Mulford, Plainfield, N. J.
Ewing, Hon. John K., Uniontown, Pa.
Ewing, Hon. Nathaniel, Uniontown, Pa.
Guerin, Mrs. Leonora D., Morristown, N. J.
Guerin, Miss Mabel T., Morristown, N. J.
Honeyman, A. V. D. (Manager), Plainfield, N. J.
Hundley, Hon. Oscar R., Huntsville, Ala.
Hundley, Mrs. Oscar R., Huntsville, Ala.
Johnson, Mr. W. J., Uniontown, Pa.
Knipe, Jacob O. M. D., Norristown, Pa.
Knipe, Mrs. Clara P., Norristown, Pa.
Mason, Mrs. E. S., New York City.
Mason, Miss Evelyn R., New York City.
Mason, Miss Adele, New York City.
Stoddard, Miss Elizabeth J., New Brunswick, N. J.
Titcomb, Miss Charlotte, Burlington, N. J.
Umbel, Mr. R. E., Uniontown, Pa.
Williams, Mrs. W. L., Paterson, N. J.
Williams, Miss Henrietta F., Paterson, N. J.

www.ingramcontent.com/pod-product-compliance
Lightning Source LLC
Chambersburg PA
CBHW020832230426
43666CB00007B/1196